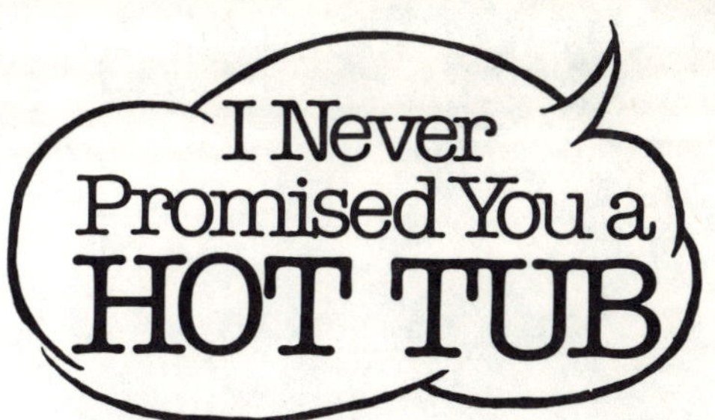
I Never
Promised You a
HOT TUB

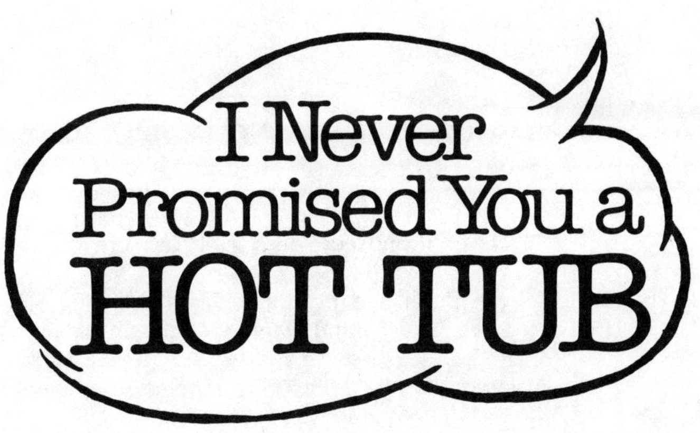

I Never Promised You a HOT TUB

Doug Peterson

Illustrated by Wayne Stayskal

Zondervan Publishing House
Grand Rapids, Michigan

I Never Promised You a Hot Tub

Daybreak Books are published by Zondervan Publishing House
1415 Lake Drive, S.E., Grand Rapids, Michigan 49506

Library of Congress Cataloging in Publication Data

Peterson, Doug
I never promised you a hot tub, and other meditations on the Beatitudes.

1. Beatititudes—Meditations. I. Title.
BT382.P45 1987 226'.9306 87-21615
ISBN 0-310-28542-9

Edited by Evelyn Bence and Julie Ackerman Link
Designed by Jerry Montague

Printed in the United States of America

88 89 90 91 92 93 94 / CH / 10 9 8 7 6 5 4 3 2

To Nancy

"Blessed is the man with a wonderful wife,
for she makes this a wonderful life."

"Blessed are the poor in spirit,
for theirs is the kingdom of heaven.
Blessed are those who mourn,
for they will be comforted.
Blessed are the meek,
for they will inherit the earth.
Blessed are those who hunger and thirst
for righteousness,
for they will be filled.
Blessed are the merciful,
for they will be shown mercy.
Blessed are the pure in heart,
for they will see God.
Blessed are the peacemakers,
for they will be called sons of God.
Blessed are those who are persecuted
because of righteousness,
for theirs is the kingdom of heaven."

MATTHEW 5:3–10

CONTENTS

PART FIVE: Blessed are the merciful, for they will be shown mercy.

PART SIX: Blessed are the pure in heart, for they will see God.

PART SEVEN: Blessed are the peacemakers, for they will be called sons of God.

PART EIGHT: Blessed are those who are persecuted because of righteousness, for theirs is the kingdom of heaven.

A BLACK BELT IN BAPTISM

AN INTRODUCTION

An elder in my church once told of a Korean he knew, a black belt in karate, who became a Christian shortly after arriving in the United States. At the man's baptism, the minister quoted Romans 6:3 before immersing him: "Don't you know that all of us who were baptized into Christ Jesus were baptized into his death?"

The Korean karate master's back stiffened almost as if he were preparing to throw the minister against the wall. Baptized into Christ's *death*? Unfamiliar with Christian expressions, the Korean thought the minister was saying he must literally die. He must *literally* drown in the baptismal.

The minister continued: "We were therefore buried with him through baptism into death in order that, just as Christ was raised from the dead through the glory of the Father, we too may live a new life."

The karate master looked out on the congregation. After a long pause his body relaxed, and the minister lowered him into the water.

The Korean rose from the water with a look of shock on his face; he had expected a literal death. And in the face of this death, he had decided to sacrifice his life, trusting that God would raise him back to life—literally.

The man had not been a Christian long, but he had enormous faith and a firm grasp on something most of us struggle all our lives to learn: Sacrifice.

Sacrifice is what the Beatitudes are all about. In baptism,

we don't have to literally sacrifice our lives, as the karate master mistakenly thought; but we *do* have to sacrifice our desire to live as we please. We must die to ourselves before we can truly live.

According to the Beatitudes, similar sacrifices result in similar blessings.

The poor in spirit sacrifice pride but gain a kingdom. Those who mourn lose something dear but gain the comfort of God. The meek give up power but gain the earth. Those who hunger for righteousness give up selfish appetites but are filled. The merciful give up the thrill of revenge but gain forgiveness. The pure in heart give up darkness but are able to see God. The peacemakers give up their craving to conquer but become sons of God. And the persecuted give up the easy life but gain the greatest life.

The Beatitudes sound like impossible standards; we cannot live by them perfectly. But we can certainly try our best. Scholar A. B. Bruce said of the Beatitudes: "We are near heaven here." And like heaven, the Beatitudes provide a lot of room for exploration. They appear simple, but once we enter into them, we come across endless rooms and passageways, attics and spiral staircases, closets and secret doorways.

The following stories do not attempt to answer any great scholarly questions about the Beatitudes, such as: "Why did Luke write 'Blessed are the poor' while Matthew wrote 'Blessed are the poor in spirit'?" But fortunately, you don't need to be a Bible scholar to explore the Beatitudes.

The door is open. Let's go in.

PART ONE

Blessed are the poor in spirit, for theirs is the kingdom of heaven.

1

A MOUNTAIN SHAMES A MOLEHILL UNTIL THEY ARE BOTH HUMBLED BY THE STARS.
(Anonymous)

In a *Peanuts* cartoon, Charlie Brown and Linus are standing next to each other, staring at a star-filled sky. "Would you like to see a falling star?" Charlie Brown asks Linus.

"Sure . . ." Linus responds. "Then again, I don't know," he adds, after some thought. "I'd hate to have it fall just on my account."

In the book *Parables of Peanuts,* Robert Short uses this cartoon to make the point that a star *did* fall on our account. God came down to us as Jesus; like a lamb led to slaughter, He died for our sakes.

Since the beginning of time, we humans have striven to be like God. This wouldn't be such a bad thing if we could just remember that being like God means we must be like Jesus—poor in spirit . . . humble.

We forget that becoming like God means we must be willing to fall like stars. It's the only way to gain the kingdom of heaven.

HORVILLE SASH
PRESIDENT

THE CAREER OF HORVILLE SASH

Once upon a time, in a city by the sea, there stood a skyscraper, spearing the clouds like a beanstalk. The company that monopolized the structure was Grindit and Co. Its specialty: bug spray.

Horville Sash worked in the lowest reaches of the building. He was a minimum-wage worker—mailroom clerk.

There came a day when Horville found a roach scurrying across the floor. As mailroom clerk, Horville had only bugs to command, to bully. He raised his foot to flatten the helpless speck.

"Spare me." The bug spoke.

"A speaking bug? Such a creature is worth millions." Visions of money cascaded through Horville's mind, splashing like a green, crisp waterfall of Washington-faced paper.

Horville spared the bug. His reward: a wish.

"I wish to be promoted to the second floor."

Granted. Horville's boss told him that very day. Horville marched up to the second floor like MacArthur and Patton rolled into one. His efficiency apartment gave way to a three-bedroom townhouse.

Wait. Horville heard footsteps on the ceiling of floor number two. There was a third floor. A higher level meant higher wages. Splashing, splashing, the visions of monetary waterfalls returned. Back to the bug. "Another wish? Are you sure?" asked the roach.

"I'm sure."

The next day, Horville rose to the third-floor post of sales coordinator. Good-by townhouse. Hello, cottage by the lake.

No use. The promotions were kerosene to a flame. Desire

grew. Burned. Horville wanted the tenth floor. He wanted to swim among the green paper portraits of presidents.

"One more wish," he said. It was done. Horville entered his tenth-floor position like a sultan on the back of an elephant. Personal secretary. Spacious office. His title: executive of sales.

His new home in the suburbs gleamed like a sword. He had cut his way to the top. But no. Can't be. Shuffling on the ceiling. More shoes, more people above his head. Higher. More rungs to the ladder. More power and money.

Back to the bug. Under threat of death, the roach granted another wish. President of sales. Horville's new office outsized his old apartment. His secretaries numbered three. "Pack your bags, wife, we're moving to Holt Estates." These were big homes, lounging like lions at the edge of suburbia.

On the elevator, Horville saw them—more numbers. More floors. More desire. Climb, climb that waterfall. The roach was summoned. Another threat. What could the bug do? Another wish. Another home. Another office.

Tragedy. A memo appeared on Horville's desk, as mysterious as a mushroom. It came from the chief executive almighty. That meant Horville wasn't on top—yet. Climb. Climb. Climb. Again, the roach was called before the sultan. "Another wish or I squash you with my penny loafers."

What could the bug do?

As chief executive almighty, Horville's domain covered six floors—ninety-four to ninety-nine. Twenty-five secretaries, all his, filed into his palace like 8 A.M.-to-5 P.M. cattle. At night their stalls were cleaned.

Horville sat by the indoor pool on floor ninety-six. The artificial wave system went out of control and tiny tidal waves raced from one end of the pool to the other. Banks of water met head-on like charging battalions. The walls echoed with the sound of splashes. The sultan laughed in the dark.

The next day, Horville discovered it by chance—a stairway leading up. "Another floor?" He scrambled up the stairs to the roof. Below him the city looked like a game of Monopoly, and the people looked like plastic pieces that he could move anywhere he chose or sweep them off the board altogether if it best suited his purposes.

He was the highest. Content, Horville headed for the stairway down. But wait. "What's this?" he said. A boy sat on the roof with his eyes closed. "What are you doing?" Horville demanded.

"Praying."

"To whom?"

Horville's wish: "To Horville."

But it wasn't so. The boy's answer: "To God."

"Who?" Horville had left his theology book in the mailroom.

The boy pointed a finger skyward. "God."

Panic gripped Horville. Was there a floor above him? He couldn't see it. Just clouds. He couldn't hear the shuffling of feet.

"Do you mean there's an authority above me?"

"Yes."

The roach was summoned.

"Roach. Make me God. Make me the highest."

"Are you sure?"

He was. "Put me in the type of position that only God would hold if He were on earth."

The very next day, Horville began work in the mailroom.

2

IN NEW YORK . . . TRINITY CHURCH STILL KEEPS WATCH OVER THE SKYSCRAPER CITY—A WARNING TO ALL WHO WOULD CONFUSE SIZE WITH GLORY, A WARNING THAT IT IS NOT HEIGHT BUT ITS POETIC POSSIBILITIES THAT INSPIRE AND ENDURE.

(Robert A. M. Stern, *The Pride of Place*)

Among cities, a major symbol of status is the skyscraper. And in the struggle for skyscraper prestige, the Chrysler Building and the Bank of the Manhattan Company Building waged one of the most intense battles in the late 1920s. Competing architects and owners kept revising their plans to ensure that their structure would be the tallest building in the world.

The bank builders thought they had the competition wrapped up when they added a lantern and a 50-foot flagpole on their structure, making it the tallest. However, as soon as the bank was completed, the Chrysler Building architect revealed a 185-foot spire that had been hidden inside the building's fire shaft. Put into place, the spire made the Chrysler Building the tallest in the world.

We struggle for status, in whatever form it appears, because we assume that being the tallest, biggest, or richest brings security. But as G. K. Chesterton points out in his book, *Francis of Assisi*, Christianity turns this notion upside down.

When we look at the world upside down, as the Beatitudes do, we see the truth. We see that humility, or poverty of spirit, brings true security.

THE UPSIDE-DOWN TOWN

At first, Mr. and Mrs. Richter didn't think anything about it. Their son, Fred, was born feet-first, instead of head-first, but a lot of babies are born that way. However, when Fred took his first step one year later, they knew something was definitely peculiar.

Fred took his first step while standing on his head instead of standing on his feet.

What's more, every time they tried to turn him right side up, he would flip back to the handstand position and begin walking around as if it were perfectly normal.

Doctors couldn't figure it out, relatives were concerned, and neighbors stared whenever little Fred would run down the sidewalk upside down.

When Fred started school, teachers tried to convince him of the benefits of standing on his feet, but Fred would not alter his topsy-turvy ways. And when it came to high-school photographs, the Huffleton High yearbook annually displayed a picture of Fred's feet amidst a sea of smiling faces.

In basketball, Fred was barred from competition because opposing players said it was annoying to have someone's smelly feet sticking in their faces whenever they went up for a rebound.

And in driver's education, Fred was declared unfit for a license because other drivers would probably be too distracted if they saw a car go by with two feet sticking up behind the steering wheel.

This was only the beginning of Fred's troubles.

Since Fred couldn't play on the basketball team, the

conference president (who happened to be his father) gave him the honor of delivering the championship trophy. But when it came time to deliver the award, Fred looked at the team standings upside down. In other words, the first-place team looked as if it were the last-place team and the last-place team looked as if it were on top of the heap.

"I can't believe it!" shouted Maury Wilbur, coach of the championship team, when he learned that Fred had given the trophy to the winless Madison Wildcats. "Have you ever heard anything crazier than the first coming last and the last coming first?"

Then it happened . . . Fred was walking through the middle of Huffleton one day when he noticed that a construction crew was clustered outside the large home of Jonathan Smith. They were in the process of converting Smith's house into a massive, mammoth, gargantuan, brick-upon-brick structure.

As if that wasn't enough, across the street Buford Jones was also adding on to his large home.

Fred gasped and immediately tracked down Mr. Smith, who was standing in his back yard with a group of architects.

"Mr. Smith, it's terrible! It's terrible what they're doing!"

"Who's doing what?" said the startled millionaire.

"Construction people say they're gonna make your house the largest in the city—even larger than Mr. Jones's house. But it's gonna fall."

"What's gonna fall?"

"If you add too much weight to your home, it'll just collapse. It's barely hanging from the sky as it is; if it gets much heavier, it'll surely fall and smash to pieces."

Mr. Smith looked puzzled for a moment, then threw back his head and began laughing. "Why, you crazy nut!" he said. "Don't you see? Because you look at things upside down, my house looks to you as if it is hanging downward. From your view, putting more weight on the house just increases the chance that it will fall from the sky. But I look at things *right side up* and realize that the more weight I put on my house, the more stability and security it has."

Fred stopped to think about this for a little while.

"But that's not right!" he burst out. "Only God gives us security. And if you'd stand on your head, just for a second, you'd see that *everything* is hanging from the sky. You'd see that God is the One who keeps it all from falling."

Fred tried to get Mr. Smith to stand on his head, but the millionaire would do nothing of the kind. "Get your hands off me, you loony. Don't you see that Mr. Jones across the street is already adding an indoor swimming pool to his house? So I've got to get busy and install my indoor swimming pool too!"

But Fred would not let up. "It's madness! You're trying to keep up with the Joneses, and Mr. Jones is trying to keep up with you, and neither one of you is trying to keep up with God."

Mr. Smith had enough. "Fred Richter, if you don't leave this instant, I'll have the police drag you away, and you can look at the world upside down from behind bars!"

"But . . . but . . ." Fred sputtered as he was escorted from the Smith property.

So the construction went on.

Mr. Jones added a gymnasium. Mr. Smith added a gymnasium. Mr. Jones added four more stories and an east wing. Mr. Smith added four more stories and an east wing. Mr. Jones added twin towers. Mr. Smith added twin towers. Mr. Jones added a sky deck. Mr. Smith added a sky deck.

Bigger and bigger and bigger—brick upon brick upon brick upon . . . CRASSSSSSHHHHHHH!

Sometime in the middle of the darkest of nights, the entire city was awakened by the thunder of shattering glass and crumbling bricks and splintering wood.

Mr. Jones's house had been the first to fall. Then, just to keep up with the Joneses, Mr. Smith's house had fallen too. But they had both fallen *up*, not down; and for one moment, everyone in town thought that maybe Fred was the one walking right side up and they were the ones with the upside-down view.

For one breath of a moment, they looked at things from Fred's perspective; they saw their city hanging upside down; they saw their dependence on God.

As G. K. Chesterton put it, they were probably thankful to God almighty that the entire cosmos had not fallen "like a vast crystal to be shattered into falling stars. Perhaps St. Peter saw the world so, when he was crucified head-downwards."

3

MANY WOULD BE SCANTILY CLAD IF CLOTHED IN THEIR HUMILITY.
(Anonymous)

In Burma, women often place numerous coils of brass around their necks—to stretch their necks for beauty's sake. But, in reality, they are smashing down their torsos. X-rays in a 1979 issue of *National Geographic* display the inner damage.

In our country we have our own destructive fashions. We sit for hours in the sun, even though it increases the risk of skin cancer; we break ankles falling from high-heeled shoes.

Just as we seem willing to sacrifice health for the sake of fashion, we are quick to sacrifice humility for the sake of fashion. "Poor in spirit" is not exactly the statement that most people make when they parade in public wearing their new outfits—outfits they probably will laugh at in five or six years.

It makes me wonder what generations in the future will think of today's fashions.

Imagine that the year is 2903 and the Interplanetary Archaeology Institute has just sent an expedition to dig up the remains of ancient civilizations on the planet Earth. The following letters are from the expedition's leader to his sponsor back on the home planet.

IN SEARCH OF ANCIENT LAUNDRY BASKETS

Salutations Master Schnitz:

We have had a breakthrough at last! We began digging in the location of an ancient village known as New York and have uncovered what these primitive people called a "laundry basket."

I'm not sure what a "basket" is, but the contraption resembles a stiff fishing net. And the "laundry" inside of it is probably fabric from some extinct animal. Judging from the decay of grime around the collar on one of these animal skins, I estimate that the laundry basket dates back to the late twentieth century.

Particularly interesting was the discovery of another device that our top scientist, Dr. Block, called "high heels." At first, I guessed that high heels were weapons capable of inflicting great pain, for they are equipped with daggerlike protrusions. I thought that the high heel was used during hand-to-hand combat, until Dr. Block informed me that they were worn on the feet!

Never having heard of feet-to-feet combat, I can't understand why anyone would wear these odd contraptions. Most likely, high heels were put on people's feet as a sadistic form of torture. More later.

Yours truly,
Dr. Bigz

Salutations Master Schnitz:

After a month of intensive study, Dr. Block concluded that these animal skins were used as clothing by the tribe in New York. Keeping in mind that these ancient people, like all people, were practical creatures, we also figured that each article of clothing must have had a purpose.

We initially believed that "socks" were worn over the nose during winter to keep that part of the face warm. But judging by the typical odor that socks give off, we later decided that these devices were kept as far from the nose as possible.

Socks, we concluded, were probably worn on the feet for several weeks and then scattered throughout the house to drive away rats and exterminate bugs.

The most interesting discovery at the site of this ancient temple (which New Yorkers called a "laundromat") were clothes known as "pants." Because each pants had two legs, and each New Yorker wore a *pair* of pants, we are led to believe that people in New York had four legs.

Dr. Block theorizes that the New Yorkers' four legs eventually evolved into two legs because it became too complicated for them to cross their legs while sitting and too time-consuming to find four matching socks every morning.

To-do-lo,
Dr. Bigz

Salutations Master Schnitz:

We are slowly unraveling the mysterious religion practiced by the New Yorkers; judging by the symbols on their clothing, I'm sorry to say that their religion was probably far from biblical.

We are now quite sure that the New York village was divided into a complex variety of religious groups, with the "preppies" serving as the ruling class. This group worshiped a great alligator god, known as Izod—the god of tweeds, polo, and upturned noses.

Another interesting sect was the "jocks," a group of people who must have had a difficult time mastering the alphabet. Even in high school and college, jocks were commonly seen wearing sweaters with letters printed on them—an obvious system for remembering what different letters of the alphabet looked like.

However, tribal worshipers in New York most commonly wore uniforms called "blue jeans" as a tribute to their many gods. The richer tribespeople often paid enormous sums of money just so they could write the name of the god Calvin Klein on the back pocket of their jeans, while lower-class tribespeople had to settle for the names of lesser gods such as Montgomery Ward.

Do you think the god Levi has any connection with the Levites of the Old Testament?

Yours,
Dr. Bigz

Salutations Master Schnitz:

I am shocked! I am appalled!

Dr. Block just discovered that all of the clothes in one of these laundry baskets were worn by only *one* person. Can you believe it? I thought for sure we had discovered the wardrobe of an entire village.

What is most distressing is that some of the New York tribespeople who worshiped at this laundromat evidently had enough clothes to keep forty people warm in winter, while other New Yorkers had barely enough clothes for their children.

According to Dr. Block, these people would hoard clothes to please the god known as Fashion. New Yorkers believed that several times a year, Fashion would gaze down from Mount Chic and declare, "Your clothes disgust me. Find something better to wear!"

The New Yorkers would scurry around buying all sorts of new clothes to appease the great, angry god; every season they would stash away their old clothes in vaults known as closets. The old clothes were sometimes given to poor New Yorkers, but most of them went to utter waste.

One of the most common excuses for spending large amounts of money on clothes was that people wanted to "make a statement to the world." But this is doubtful because most New

Yorkers were capable of clear speech (except for a group known as "lawyers"). So why did they need to use clothes to make a statement?

Sometimes they even bought elaborate, high-priced costumes just to change their images. If some man wanted to feel like a rough-and-tumble cowboy, he simply dressed as a cowboy; if a woman wanted to feel young, she dressed as Little Bo-Peep.

Instead of *acting* like the people they wanted to be, they found it easier to *dress* like they wanted to be.

But Jesus said, "And why do you worry about clothes? See how the lilies of the field grow. They do not labor or spin. Yet I tell you that not even Solomon in all his splendor was dressed like one of these" (Matt. 6:28).

By the way, I think we finally figured out the purpose of a hair net. Bald men used it like a fishing net, casting for hair in local barbershops.

Give my best to the wife and children.

Toodles,
Dr. Bigz

PART TWO

Blessed are those who mourn, for they will be comforted.

SAD SOUL, TAKE COMFORT NOR FORGET,
THE SUNRISE NEVER FAILED US YET.
(Celia Laighton Thaxter)

When Father Damien entered a muddy hut on the Hawaiian island of Molokai, the smell nearly knocked him over. A leper lay on a wet mat, the decaying remains of his hands clutching a prayer book.

With holy oil, this nineteenth-century missionary anointed the man's eyes, ears, and nose. As he proceeded to the feet, he noticed that the skin on the man's legs appeared to move. Father Damien quickly realized that worms were eating away at the man's body. With growing nausea, he finished the ritual. And by the time the sun set, the man was dead.

Even in the midst of such horror, the comfort of God remained with that man. His mother, having witnessed the comfort God brought to her son and sensing her own approaching death, asked Father Damien for the same peace. Two hours after she was baptized, she died.

Blessed are those who mourn, for they will find comfort. English writer John Stott points out that "blessed" can be translated as "happy." Consequently, "blessed are those who mourn" can be interpreted as "happy are the unhappy." The puzzling nature of this beatitude is probably why many of us prefer a simpler but contradictory principle. Instead of believing "blessed are those who mourn, for they will find comfort," we prefer "blessed are those who are comfortable, for they shall not mourn."

It's tempting to believe we can find comfort soaking in a hot tub, rather than soaking in God's presence.

I Never Promised You a Hot Tub

I NEVER PROMISED YOU A HOT TUB

"Knock and the door will be opened to you."
—Jesus

"Knock heads and the door will be opened to you."
—Jimmy Wiffo

A rock clunked against the side of Pastor Rose's car as he wheeled into the church parking lot. Then, with two armed guards escorting him, he pushed his way through the shouting crowd.

"Pastor Rose, the Christians in your church are into the fourth week of their strike," said a television announcer, sticking a microphone within inches of the preacher's mouth. "When do you think it will end?"

Before Pastor Rose had a chance to answer, two other reporters lunged at him with questions.

"Is there any hope that the American Federation of Liturgy–Christian Industrial Organization (AFL-CIO) will put an end to their prayer stoppage today?"

"Tell us, pastor, what did you think when union leaders tried to halt all conversions in your church yesterday?"

"I was disgusted that anyone wishing to answer an altar call had to cross a picket line first," the pastor responded. "That's why I had my assistant ask people to show their new commitment to Christ by simply raising their hands."

"Your assistant? Doesn't he have union sympathies?"

"Yes, but I didn't know it at the time. I was stunned when he began saying to newly committed Christians, 'Yes, I see that scab. And yes, I see *that* scab.' "

I Never Promised You a Hot Tub

As another television camera pushed its way out of the crowd, Pastor Rose stopped and sighed. He hoped that if he answered a few more questions, they might leave him alone.

"Is it true," said one reporter, "that there is the risk of sympathy strikes from other unions—the International Redeemsters Union, the Michael-Row-the-Boat-Ashoreman's Union, and the United Shrine Workers, to be specific?"

"Yes, it's always a risk."

"Do you think it was wise to bring in the national guard?"

"By all means. Without the national guard, we wouldn't have been able to keep the church rolling. Who else would've collected offerings, taught Sunday school classes, and held bake sales?"

"Pastor, is it true that strikers have been taking pot-shots at church buses and slashing choir robes?"

"No comment. I'm sorry, but that's all the time I have."

The journalists persisted with their flurry of questions while the pastor motioned them off and rushed into the church building. Inside, he was scheduled to face Christian union leaders at the bargaining table.

"Okay, pastor, are you prepared to make some concessions yet?" asked Jimmy Wiffo, union leader and author of *Scab Christians in an Age of Unions*.

Pastor Rose threw up his arms. "All right, all right, you win. I'll agree to let members of the International Trespasses Brotherhood recite 'Forgive us our trespasses' during the Lord's Prayer, even though the rest of the church says 'Forgive us our debts.' "

"That's your only concession?" Wiffo growled. "We want more than that. We're tired of the pitiful working conditions that you insist are part of a normal Christian life. Your requirements are totally out of line!"

Pastor Rose loosened his tie and noticed that the room was getting stuffy. Pressure. It was the pressure. "What do you think is out of line?"

"First of all," Wiffo said, shuffling through his list of

demands, "what's all this about devoting our *entire* life to Christ? Isn't it a little extreme to expect us to put in a 168-hour work week as Christians?"

"No, because I think—"

"We insist on ten-hour work weeks. For the rest of the week, we get to act like heathens."

"Yes, but—"

"Second, we think the fringe benefits are deplorable. Take spiritual sick leave, for example. After all of our hard work, we deserve three weeks of backsliding time per year."

"Okay, I can see that—"

"And during every church service, we want two fifteen-minute breaks so church members can go to the lunch room to smoke, gamble, and dance—things they can't do while they're on the job."

"Yes, but—"

"And if anyone should become apostate while on the job, he should get churchman's compensation. It's only fair."

"Churchman's compensation? Now that's going a little too—"

"Being a Christian is a pretty dangerous calling, so we're also asking that you make our spiritual work environment a little safer. We insist that all people who roll in the aisles be equipped with either roll bars or air bags so they don't hurt themselves."

"Surely, you're not implying—"

"I'm not finished yet. Our medical benefits are in dire need of improvement. We demand that all prayers for healing be answered within four hours, and we insist on time-and-a-half for praying after hours, compensation for 'kneeler's knee,' and yearly raises that keep up with the rising cost of discipleship."

"That does it!" Pastor Rose shouted, jumping to his feet. "For your information, Jesus never said the Christian life would be a plush venture with wall-to-wall fringe benefits. In fact, He guaranteed a rough go of it. He called us to be like the mustard seed that falls into the ground and dies."

"Sorry, but that's out of the question," Wiffo countered.

"I'm not a member of the United Brotherhood of Mustard Seeds, so I couldn't fall into the ground and die even if I wanted to."

"Well . . . can't you at least dig the holes or water the seeds?"

"No can do. I'm not a card-carrying member of the Seed-Hole-Diggers Union or the International Fellowship of Seed Sprinklers, so my life would be at risk if I dared to take their jobs. Which reminds me—in our latest list of demands, we insist that before we die, God must give us the vacation time we earned and at least a thirty-day notice. We'd also like to see the problem of evil solved and our church equipped with recliner pews. And then we'd like—"

"I know what you're trying to do!" Pastor Rose shouted, leveling a finger at Wiffo. "You're trying to pass an antitrust law, aren't you? By making everything comfortable and easy, you're trying to eliminate the need to trust God. Maybe if you were living in Bangladesh or Ethiopia, you'd realize how soft you have it here."

All at once, the room filled with silence.

Pastor Rose stood back, wiped the perspiration from his brow, and waited for his words to settle inside the mind of Jimmy Wiffo. The labor leader appeared to be deep in thought. Could it be that the words of Pastor Rose had made a mark in his mind? Could it be?

"Bangladesh or Ethiopia?" mused Wiffo, stroking his chin and staring into space.

With breathless suspense, Pastor Rose nodded. Another silence. A long-stretching silence.

Suddenly, Wiffo slapped his knee and declared, "Boy, am I glad you brought that up, Pastor Rose. I almost forgot to demand that all multi-national churches stop sending resources overseas. Money should stay in this country where we can put it to important uses—maybe build a hot tub or an artificial wave system so we can go body surfing in the baptismal.

"And while I'm on the subject," he continued, "anyone who chooses to be born again deserves a four-month maternity leave—five months if taken by cesarean. Also, we think the Ten Commandments are much too strict and should be called the Ten Suggestions. And about that Sermon on the Mount . . ."

It was time to call in a mediator between management and labor, someone to span the gap between the Lord of the Universe and the lords of this world.

5

SIN, EVERY DAY, TAKES OUT A NEW PATENT FOR SOME NEW INVENTION.
(Edwin Percy Whipple)

People who mourn over their excess weight have been known to go to ridiculous lengths (and widths) to shed pounds. For example, *The Great American Waistline* tells of a mail-order outfit that advertised Slim-Skins—plastic pants with a hose sticking out. Simply connect the hose to a vacuum cleaner, start the vacuum, and (according to claims) it will remove two-and-one-half inches from your waist, four inches from your stomach, two inches from your hips, and three inches from each thigh in just twenty-five minutes.

If you don't believe that, try Obesity Ointment, which allegedly removes fat when you apply it to your body. If that doesn't work, there is the Diet Conscience—a recording that lambastes you with such statements as, "Are you eating again? Shame on you! No wonder you look the way you do! Ha! Ha! Ha! You'll be sorry, fatty!" every time you open the refrigerator.

Many people react to sins the same way they react to excess pounds. They begin by mourning over their sins, which can be the first step toward God. But then come the problems. Just as many people resort to drastic measures when trying to remove excess weight, they often resort to drastic measures when trying to remove sin.

In reality, the only measure necessary for shedding the guilt of sin is asking God for forgiveness. But we have a knack for avoiding simple solutions. We prefer to *earn* God's love by performing works and rituals. We would rather burn away sins by our own effort than find comfort in our Lord's forgiveness. The result is "sin-losing diets" such as these.

I LOST THREE THOUSAND SINS IN ONE DAY!

The Complete Hare-Scarsdale Metaphysical Diet. This diet is popular among followers of many Eastern religions, who believe that whenever you commit sins, you build up bad karma—or "karmahydrates" as they are known in the diet biz. They believe the only way to rid yourself of bad karma is by doing good works and chanting, "Hare Scarsdale, Hare Scarsdale, Scarsdale, Scarsdale, Hare, Hare."

By earning enough "good karma," you supposedly will be reincarnated into a higher life form, such as a food taster at a chocolate factory. But if you do not earn enough "good karma," you may come back as a person whose profession is to travel from restaurant to restaurant eating unwanted parsley.

The Sun Moon Simmons Never Say Diet Program. Various cults have picked up on this sin-losing technique in a big way. This program offers a series of strenuous exercises in which cult followers flex their leg and mouth muscles by jogging door-to-door to sell flowers, candles, and other assorted goods.

Cult members are asked to give up their money, time, and identity; in return, they are given an exercise manual that helps them burn away thousands of sins.

One popular exercise, commonly practiced in airports, is the "one-handed money lift." It goes like this:

"Inhale deep, one-two-three-four, and approach a stranger. Exhale and thrust your right hand forward, clutching a flower tightly. Then exercise your jaw muscles rigorously, one-two-three-four, and ask if they would buy a flower to save all humanity. (However, be sure not to mention that your 'leader' plans to spend 90 percent of the money on new carpeting, a pilgrimage to the Bahamas, and braces for his pet hamster's teeth.) When money has been placed in your hand, one-two-three-four, thrust your arm back; and with a downward motion, place it in your pocket. Release money, one-two-three-four. Repeat seven thousand times daily."

Although the preceding two diets are used mainly by cults, I should note that Christians have strange sin-losing diets of their own—diets such as these:

The Beverly Hills Theological Diet. This program boasts that it is the first guilt-free diet. "Yes, you can have your cake and stuff your face too!" says an advertisement for the Beverly Hills Theological Diet.

Advocates of this program claim that you can be as greedy and as irritable and as gluttonous and as lustful and as prideful as you like, and you don't have to worry about whether you're sinning or not. After all, God will forgive all of your sins, won't He?

There also are slight variations on this diet. For example, one Beverly Hills dietitian says that the average American commits 1,200 sins per day, and only after you exceed this "average daily intake" will you begin to collect fatty sin deposits on your soul.

In addition, the same Beverly Hills dietitian devised a chart showing that the amount and type of sins you can commit depends on your height. By consulting a height-sin chart, for instance, you will find that a person under six feet tall will be unable to commit certain sins, such as scribbling nasty language on basketball backboards.

One of the many side-effects of the Beverly Hills Theological Diet, though, is that you commonly find that your salt has lost its flavor.

Pastor Atkins' Diet Revolution. Instead of helping you lose sins, this program puts you on a strict world-free diet to keep you from committing sins in the first place.

Avoiding sins is a great idea, of course, but this diet suggests that you do so by cutting off *all* contact with the world.

For example, here is a daily menu for a person using the Diet Revolution:

"Breakfast—Sit up in bed. Turn your head slightly to the left, but be sure it does not cause you to sin. Lunch—By this time, it is probably safe to blink three times. Dinner—For the rest of the evening, you are allotted four yawns, two sneezes, and one low-sodium hiccup."

If you abide by this diet, Pastor Atkins says you are guaranteed to remain pure, for how can you commit a sin if you never do anything but sit up, blink, sneeze, yawn, and hiccup?

6

CHRIST HAS MADE OF DEATH A NARROW, STARLIT STRIP BETWEEN THE COMPANIONSHIPS OF YESTERDAY AND THE REUNIONS OF TOMORROW.

(William Jennings Bryan)

People often suffer from mid-life crises because they see youth slipping away. I propose, therefore, that children help parents recapture their childlike spirit by giving them toys such as Barbie and Ken mid-life dolls that lose their hair and beauty, as well as their identities. Or maybe children could tell parents stories about "the denture fairy," who leaves mutual funds under pillows in exchange for lost teeth.

Okay, so maybe these aren't the best solutions. But the fact remains: Many people suffer from mid-life crises because they mourn their vanishing youth.

Whenever we lose something, whether it is a loved one or our youth, mourning is natural and often therapeutic. But many people in the grip of a mid-life crisis go beyond therapeutic mourning and become obsessed with the fear of death.

I once read that the word *coffin* was originally used to describe any type of basket or basketlike chest. An English dictionary in 1542 used that very word in saying that Moses was placed in a "coffyn" and placed amidst reeds along the Nile River. Hidden in his coffin, so to speak, baby Moses escaped the wrath of Pharaoh.

And if we turn to God, we too can escape. We can escape the wrath of Death, a figure as fearful as any Pharaoh. When our earthly lives are over—when we are placed in a basket and hidden in the ground—we too will be rescued, plucked from the reeds by a Father Who wants to raise us as sons and daughters.

Are we willing to accept His comfort?

AN APPOINTMENT WITH DEATH

"What seems to be your problem?" asked the psychiatrist.

"Nobody likes me," said Death, a ghastly figure who was stretched out on the psychiatrist's couch. "Whenever I go near people, they run away in terror. I haven't been invited to an Optimist's Club meeting for twenty years—just because my favorite discussion topics happen to be disease, war, and nuclear holocaust."

"How long have you felt this way, Mr. Death?"

"You can call me Die. I prefer to be informal."

"Okay . . . . How long have you felt this way . . . Die?"

"Ever since I arrived on this planet, back when Adam and Eve were running around. Did you know that a tall, dark, and gruesome guy like me hasn't had a date in four thousand years? Girls don't like the kiss of Death. They won't even shake hands with me."

"Go with that thought, Mr. Death."

"Just last month I held a garage sale because I was trying to sell some old grim-reaper sickles and a few dead doornails. But my neighbors were too afraid to come by and browse."

"My, this *is* serious."

"The last straw snapped last week when my boss sent me over to see Mr. Grolley, president of the First United Bank."

"Would you like to tell me about it?"

Death took a deep breath, looked at the ceiling, and nodded. Then he began his tale. "As I headed toward the door to Mr. Grolley's office," Death explained, "his secretary stopped me and said that I couldn't see him without an appointment.

"When I told her that I had an appointment at noon, she

reminded me that it was only eight o'clock in the morning. So, I then tried to explain that Mr. Grolley was scheduled to be hit by a car at noon. But if I could take him away now—four hours early—he could leave this life without having to go through that terrible car accident.

"The secretary gave me the most perplexed gaze that I ever saw and then pushed her intercom button. 'Who should I say is calling?' she asked, and I loudly declared, 'My name is Death.'

"Several people standing nearby ran out of the bank screaming, but the secretary kept her cool. She pushed her intercom switch and said, 'Mr. Grolley, Death is here to see you.' There was a long pause at the other end of the intercom and then a garbled voice said, 'Tell him I'm out to lunch.'

"The secretary pointed out to Mr. Grolley that eight o'clock in the morning was a little early for lunch, and he said, 'Oh . . . then tell Death that I'll be with him as soon as I'm done with a client.'

"The secretary suggested that I take a seat, and I did just that," Death continued. "But about ten minutes later, a bizarre character came walking out of Mr. Grolley's office. He was dressed in the wildest punk outfit you can imagine—torn, ill-fitting, purple-and-pink clothes—and his hair was orange and maroon. 'I'll see you later, Mr. Grolley,' the punk shouted; then he headed for the bank exit in an unusual hurry.

"I wasn't fooled for a moment. I knew the punk was really Mr. Grolley in a youthful disguise. This happens all the time. People think that if they pretend to be young, they won't have to face Death.

"Anyway," Death said to the psychiatrist, "I stood up in the waiting room, pointed a long, narrow finger at the punk, and shouted, 'You can't trick me. You're Mr. Grolley!'

" 'No, I'm not,' he insisted. And then, to prove he was just a young guy off the street, Mr. Grolley fell to the floor and tried to do some break dancing. But about all that he broke were three lamps, a coffee table, and one arm.

"After realizing that I wasn't going to be convinced, Mr.

Grolley bolted out the door, and I ended up chasing him through a park, a zoo, and four museums. I lost track of him on the subway system but, a couple of hours later, I found him at a restaurant, where he was having a business lunch.

"This time, Mr. Grolley tried another age-old tactic to evade me. He pretended that I didn't even exist. He simply ignored me and acted as if Death were someone who only visited other people.

"Well . . . by this time I had had enough, so I grabbed Mr. Grolley by the collar and pulled him from his chair. But do you know what that crazy guy kept doing? He continued to ignore me.

"Even though I was pulling him across the carpet, he continued to chat with people. As I dragged him through the non-smoking section, he recognized someone and shouted, 'Hi, Kevin. How are the wife and kids?' And as I lugged him out the door, he looked up at the waiter and chirped, 'See you tomorrow, Nick. Racquetball at seven o'clock . . . right?'

"Not until I dragged him outside to the curb did Mr. Grolley finally recognize that ignoring Death would do him no good. He panicked, thrashed around like a hooked fish, wrestled his way free, and dashed across the street. That's when I heard a car horn and the screech of tires. Mr. Grolley never made it across the street. It was noon.

"So you see," said Death to the psychiatrist, "people are terrified of me. Even those who think they're not afraid of me are, way down deep. As Woody Allen once said, 'I'm not afraid to die. I just don't want to be there when it happens.' "

"I see. . . . Go on, go on."

"It makes me wonder why some people actually choose to face me *alone*, rather than with someone like God at their side." Death paused, sighed, and added, "I just wish somebody, for once, would be friendly to me. Say, Doc, what are you doing for lunch today?"

"Oh my, look at the time," the psychiatrist suddenly shouted. "I gotta get going!"

"But there's a great restaurant down the street where I

know the waiter personally. Whenever he asks how I like my steak, I tell him that I like it dead, and we have a good laugh. How about it?"

"Sorry. I really gotta get going."

"Well . . . Can't I at least set another appointment?"

The psychiatrist shuffled nervously through his appointment book. "Uh . . . sure, I'll set an appointment. Let's see, I'm booked up for a while, but . . . Yes, I think I have an opening in fifty years."

"Fifty years?"

"Yeah, come back and see me when I'm gray-haired and unable to walk across the room."

"But . . ."

"Gotta go. See you later."

In two seconds, the psychiatrist had grabbed his coat and hat and sprinted out the door like a man running for dear life.

PART THREE

Blessed are the meek, for they will inherit the earth.

THE PROUD MAN COUNTS HIS NEWSPAPER CLIPPINGS—THE HUMBLE MAN HIS BLESSINGS.

(Bishop Fulton J. Sheen)

Leo Tolstoy wrote a short story about a bishop who visited a tiny island where three poor, uneducated men of God lived alone. The three old men knew only one prayer, "Three are Ye, three are we, have mercy on us!"

"I see you wish to please the Lord, but you do not know how," said the bishop. "That is not the way to pray." So the bishop spent the day teaching the men the Lord's Prayer. They learned slowly, but by night they could recite the prayer.

Hours after the bishop had said farewell to the men and set sail for home, he and his crew saw what they thought was a ship sailing after them. They soon realized, though, that it was, as Tolstoy put it, the "three hermits running upon the water, all gleaming white, their gray beards shining, and approaching the ship as quickly as though it were not moving." Stopping within shouting distance of the ship, the hermits called to the bishop. They had forgotten the Lord's Prayer and wanted him to teach them the words again.

Humbled by the faith of these men, the bishop told them their own prayer would reach the Lord. "It is not for me to teach," he said. "Pray for us sinners."

Meekness means total dependence on God—a quality the bishop saw in these men. They had the faith to run across waves, yet they did not do it to impress others; they did it to ask for more teaching.

The hermits had few clothes and very little intelligence, but they were meek enough to know they had all they needed.

So did Clifton O'Connor. He was a shepherd.

I Never Promised You a Hot Tub

MARY HAD A LITTLE LAMB
(AND A BIG CORPORATION)

The old nursery rhyme says that "Mary had a little lamb." However, it fails to mention that Mary was a shrewd businesswoman who soon expanded her operation to forty lambs.

After taking over a competitor, Sheep Unlimited, her company boasted a total of 234 sheep. And when she swallowed up a nationwide rent-a-shepherd corporation, she found herself with over 30,000 sheep.

It didn't take long before another string of takeovers and a few nicely maneuvered mergers left her owning every single sheep in the world . . . except for thirty which were owned by Clifton O'Connor, a simple shepherd who roamed the hillsides.

Mary desperately wanted those final thirty sheep. She wanted complete control.

"Okay, you can send in Mr. O'Connor," Mary told her secretary one afternoon. A man wearing a worn jacket and carrying a shepherd's staff ambled into her glass-paneled office. Three sheep followed close behind.

"Excuse the mud," Mr. O'Connor said, taking off his shoes.

"Oh, don't worry about it," Mary said. "I have new carpeting installed every week anyway." Then she told the shepherd to take a seat. "So what is it, Mr. O'Connor? Do you want more money? Is that why you won't sell your sheep to me?"

"Oh no," said the shepherd, smiling. "I have all the money I care to be burdened with. I just wanna keep shepherding."

Mary offered him a cigar, but Mr. O'Connor declined. "Then why don't you sell me your sheep and shepherd for *my* company? We have great benefits: forty vacation days every year, use of the company hot tubs, and excellent wolf insurance. Whatya think?"

Mr. O'Connor stared at his worn hands. "Well, I just—"

Before the shepherd could get his words out, a man barged into the office and shouted, "Mary! I have the perfect slogan for our new advertising campaign! Just listen . . . 'A heap of sheep is cheap!' Well . . . do you like it? Catchy, huh?"

Mary responded with a stony gaze. "Can't you see that I have a guest?"

The advertising man glanced at the shepherd, muttered his apology, and slipped from the room.

"You were saying, Mr. O'Connor?"

The old shepherd continued to stare at his hands. "Well, Mary, I really don't want to shepherd for you. Your employees don't seem willing to lay down their lives for their sheep."

"Well of course not!" Mary exclaimed. "Do you know how much it costs to train a new shepherd? We have too much invested to have our shepherds tossing away their lives for a few sheep. It's not good business!"

"But it says in John 10:11 that a good shepherd gives his life for his sheep. And it says in John 10:3 that a good shepherd calls his sheep by name. Do the shepherds in your company call their sheep by name?"

Mary propped her feet on her desk. "Yeah, they call them by names . . . in a way. They call them X456, Y357, or Z298."

"Those are numbers, not names."

"So who cares?" Mary sighed. "It's a lot easier to take inventory if we number our sheep."

Trying to take the offensive, Mary changed the subject and blabbed all about her company's recent innovations. For example, they just began a new sales campaign in which shepherds sell sheep door-to-door; they developed chocolate-flavored grass for sweet-toothed sheep; and they created new miniature sheep. The miniature sheep were so small that an entire flock could fit into a briefcase—perfect for shepherds who commute to work.

"So whatya say, O'Connor? Wanna join our great outfit?"

The shepherd smiled, pulled a Bible from his satchel, and posed a question for Mary. "If one of the sheep in a herd of one hundred became lost, Mary, what would you do?"

"Oh, that's easy," she said. "We'd let it stay lost and write it off as a tax deduction."

"See! That's another reason why I couldn't work for your company. A good shepherd would leave the other ninety-nine sheep and search for the one lost lamb. And if he found the lost sheep, he would have a big celebration."

"On company time?"

"Yes. On company time."

"That's crazy!" Mary exploded. "You'd go off looking for one measly little lamb? That's not good business!"

"But that's how God runs our world," Mr. O'Connor said. "No matter how lost we become, He will come to look for us. And when He rescues us, there is a celebration in heaven."

"On company time?"

"Yes. On company time."

"Well, if I were God, I'd hire a quality control expert and let the most corrupt sinners rot in their juices. I'd only concentrate on cost-effective people—people who are purer than pure."

"Jesus ate with sinners," Mr. O'Connor reminded her.

"But that's bad business. So whatya say, my friend? Do you wanna become part of our *good* business and collect a hundred thousand dollars a year? Just sign on the old dotted line and . . ."

Mr. O'Connor stood up. "I'm sorry, Mary, but I gotta be going. My other twenty-seven sheep are browsing in the gift shop downstairs, and I shouldn't keep them waiting."

"But you haven't signed on the dotted line. You haven't agreed to sell your sheep to me yet!"

With a burst of panic, Mary tried every possible ploy. She

promised him an office overlooking the ocean, and she promised him a share of profits from the company's other enterprises—sheep movies, sheep restaurants, and sheep dolls. She even promised to give him a lifetime supply of toy sheep that you wind up and place on your head. That way, they graze on your hair and give you a haircut in the process.

But for every promise that she made, Mr. O'Connor quoted a better promise made by God. "The way God runs the world might not be very good business," the old man said. "But it is very good shepherding."

Within a half-hour, Mr. O'Connor was back on a hillside, caring for his thirty sheep.

8

IF GOD WOULD CONCEDE ME HIS OMNIPOTENCE FOR TWENTY-FOUR HOURS, YOU WOULD SEE HOW MANY CHANGES I WOULD MAKE IN THE WORLD. BUT IF HE GAVE ME HIS WISDOM TOO, I WOULD LEAVE THINGS AS THEY ARE.
(J. M. L. Monsabre)

In the early 1960s, the following obituary appeared in a Methodist student magazine:

> Atlanta, GA—God, creator of the universe, principal deity of the world's Jews, ultimate reality of Christians, the most eminent of all divinities, died late yesterday during major surgery undertaken to correct a massive diminishing influence.

This obituary was a byproduct of what was known as the "Death of God" movement—a short-lived movement built on the premise that God had lost all impact on our secular Western society.

It is also a good example of human arrogance. If we humans aren't telling God that He has died, we're telling Him to stay out of public schools and off of other public property. (Any day now, I expect the old folk song to be revised to say, "He's got the whole world, except public property, in His hands. He's got the whole world, except public property, in His hands.")

What's more, if we're not telling Him to stay off of public property, we're usually telling Him how to run the world.

The meek shall inherit the earth; but if many people had their way, they would probably forget the inheritance from God and start building their own planet.

Maybe then they would get the type of world they always wanted. Or would they?

CREATING A MESS

THE FIRST DAY

In the beginning, two characters named Marvin and Larry decided to create their own planet because they were tired of being submissive to God. They wanted to run their own business.

Larry, for example, thought he could do a much better job than God in all sorts of areas, such as creating leaves. Larry thought he would create leaves with legs—to cut down on raking every fall. With just a little nudge, the leaves would obediently walk into the leaf bags on their own, eliminating all of the back-breaking work.

When Larry and Marvin began their project, the earth was formless and void, kind of like most of the shows you see on television. And Larry said, "Let there be light." Actually, he said, "Give me a light," but nothing happened. After six failed attempts at creating light, Larry decided to order light from a catalog. And it was done. Unfortunately, light broke down after it had been in use only ten minutes. "Let there be warranties," said Marvin. And it was okay—the first day.

THE SECOND DAY

On the second day, Larry rested. Marvin called him up and asked when he was showing up for work, but Larry said he deserved a vacation day. Creating light took everything out of him. Marvin invented name-calling and slammed down the phone. And it was not okay any more.

Work was piling up, so Marvin hired a few inexperienced assistants to create the sky. Unfortunately, one of them accidentally punctured the atmosphere and let all the air out of it.

After Marvin spent the rest of the day patching the atmosphere, he suddenly realized that his hired help had installed the sky upside down. In other words, outer space was nearest to earth and the blue sky was out where outer space was supposed to be.

With the sky upside down, gravity was reversed. What went up didn't come down. Instead, what came down went up. Making the appropriate repairs led to a long night for Marvin. And it was getting tiring. The second day.

THE THIRD DAY

Marvin decided to give Larry a taste of his own medicine. He called in sick, even though he felt perfectly fine. That left Larry with all of the work—ordering fungi, putting seeds in fruit, and attaching stingers to bees.

Larry was unable to find any wings to attach to birds, so he bought them airline tickets instead. Then, when a leaky cloud became annoying, he hired a plumber who charged him five billion dollars for labor alone. In the evening, Larry decided that he better create bankers because he needed to take out a loan.

And it was getting expensive. The third day.

THE FOURTH DAY

Larry decided they should receive credit for their remarkable creation, so he arranged the stars in such a way that they spelled out the words, "This world was brought to you by Larry and Marvin."

When Marvin spotted this arrangement of stars, he made sure Larry wasn't around and then shuffled them to say, "This world was brought to you by Marvin and Larry."

Later on, Larry discovered that Marvin had mistakenly attached all of the bird wings to elephants, and he became steaming mad. Evidently, flying elephants had been causing all sorts of trouble by trying to land on small bird-feeders and by building nests in trees that could not carry their weight. Worst of all, elephants had been flying into people's picture windows.

That's when Larry noticed that Marvin had rearranged the stars to say, "This world was brought to you by Marvin and Larry," instead of "Larry and Marvin."

Larry invented the punch in the nose. And it was painful. The fourth day.

THE FIFTH DAY

On the fifth day, they procrastinated and got nothing done. And it was getting out of hand.

THE SIXTH DAY

On the sixth day, paperwork was invented. Larry was informed that the check he used to pay for four billion amoebas had bounced. In addition, the power bill to keep the sun running was exorbitant, so he decided to keep the sun running only two minutes out of every day.

The result of this cost-cutting measure was a flood of prayers from the people they had created. The people pleaded for more sunlight.

The number of prayers Larry and Marvin received that day was so enormous, they hired a secretary and told her to answer prayers with a form letter. The letter said:

> Dear Sir/Madam:
>
> Thank you for submitting your prayer. Unfortunately, your prayer does not suit our purposes at the present time. Good luck with all future endeavors. Sincerely, your creators.

To raise some desperately needed money, Marvin created toll booths every five feet on their planet's surface and every six feet underwater, but it still wasn't enough to cover their debts. During the evening, the bank told Larry and Marvin that if they didn't pay their bills, their oceans would be confiscated.

As a last-ditch effort, Larry decided to hold a telephone fund-raising campaign known as Create-athon. The number to call to pledge support for your planet was 756-0394. That number again is . . .

Meanwhile, Marvin traveled to another solar system to see if he could borrow money there, but the entire universe had found out about their bad credit. He couldn't even find anybody who would accept his Creator's Express Card ("Don't create home without it").

Finally, their last hope was dashed. Larry's pet project—his leaves with legs—had backfired. His newfangled leaves were even *harder* to rake up than normal leaves. Whenever you nudged them with a rake, they sprinted in another direction, laughing and calling you names.

The sixth day.

THE SEVENTH DAY

On the seventh day, Larry and Marvin's ramshackle planet went out of business. And it was a mess.

9

WHEN A JEW CEASED FROM HIS LABOR [ON THE SABBATH], A LITTLE ETERNITY INVADED HIS LIFE. HE DWELT NO LONGER IN THE KINGDOM OF NECESSITY, BUT LIVED FOR A FEW HOURS IN THE FREEDOM OF THE COMING KINGDOM.
(Ben Patterson)

When the Ringling Brothers and Barnum and Bailey Chapel rolls into town, be sure to see the greatest death-defying feat of all: Gideon Sterling, the fabulous human torch.

"To your astonishment," says the chapel's press release, "the human torch will try to juggle a full-time job, a family of seven, a place on the church softball team, five hobbies, two Bible studies, a prayer group, and a position on twelve church committees; and then he will burn out right in front of your eyes!"

Whether we crowd our lives with church activities or employment, we often have one problem: We do not understand meekness. We do not understand our limitations.

Instead, we act as if we believe we can do it all and have it all, so we grab for it all. In the process, we lose what is most important. Instead of inheriting the earth, we lose it in a frenzy of activity.

To someone with out-of-control ambition, the Sabbath rest can be one bothersome idea.

THE LEGEND OF REV. VAN WINKLE

People used to say that laziness ran in the Van Winkle blood—or at least it "walked in their blood." (Van Winkle blood would never do any running, unless absolutely necessary.)

Well, Rev. Jeremiah Van Winkle, a descendant of the famed Rip Van Winkle, was determined to put an end to the family reputation. By kindergarten, he had his first taste of solid work; when he entered high school, he was a closet workaholic.

"I should have suspected that he was a workaholic," Van Winkle's wife would later tell friends. "After all, he didn't even show up for our wedding because he had seminary work to do."

To the embarrassment of Mrs. Van Winkle's entire family, she had to stand at the altar with a message recorder that said, "I'm sorry, I can't be at my wedding today. After the tone, please leave your name and wedding vows, and I will get back to you as soon as possible."

After the minister declared them "message recorder and wife," Mrs. Van Winkle tucked the machine under her arm, dashed from the chapel, and began the honeymoon. Jeremiah Van Winkle couldn't make the honeymoon, but he sent along a life-sized cardboard replica of himself so his wife would have something to pose with in the photographs.

With a history like this, Mrs. Van Winkle should not have been surprised that her husband was sucked into the black hole of overcommitment when he was ordained and put in charge of a church. As a part of his weekly routine, Rev. Van Winkle would write two sermons, lead three Bible studies, chair twelve committees, serve as the host of a local radio show, counsel twenty people, attend choir practice, coordinate the building program, and referee two squabbles.

On Tuesdays, his schedule was even busier.

One day, Rev. Van Winkle found himself with ten minutes of free time—an unheard-of situation for a workaholic like him. So he decided to dash to his publisher's office to find out if any galleys needed to be proofread. He wanted to consume that extra ten minutes in a fireball of energy. Relaxation was out of the question.

As if ten minutes of free time weren't exasperating enough, Rev. Van Winkle found himself wasting an entire half-hour by getting lost. He made a right turn on Kaatskill Avenue and, expecting to see a large, dark-glass building looming over him, he encountered a row of old but well-maintained buildings.

When Rev. Van Winkle turned to retrace his steps, someone called out, "Rev. Van Winkle! Rev. Van Winkle!"

The voice seemed to be coming from a small pub. Rev. Van Winkle was hesitant to investigate, but curiosity got the best of him and he walked through the doorway. Inside the pub, he found a small man who slapped him on the back and shouted, "Welcome to the workaholic bar!"

The workaholic bar was a poorly lit place where customers sat on stools and did paperwork, dictated memos, or busied themselves in any way possible.

"Give me a double," the small man told the bartender. "And do the same for my friend here."

"Oh no, I couldn't—" Rev. Van Winkle started to say, but the man interrupted him with another slap on the back.

"What's wrong, my friend? Doesn't the wife let you stop in for nips of paperwork?"

"No, I mean yes, but . . ."

With a thump, the bartender dropped a stack of paperwork on the bar—paperwork that came complete with a lemon stapled to the top sheet. It was Friday evening, a time when the tavern routinely held Unhappy Hour, and when workaholics gathered for an all-you-can-sweat work session.

At first, Rev. Van Winkle was cautious about touching the stuff set down before him. But after one taste of the work, he was hooked. The paperwork they served was the most intoxicating kind; by the time Rev. Van Winkle had polished off his first stack of paperwork, the adrenalin was really flowing.

"I'll have another, bartender!" he shouted. "In fact, paperwork all around!"

The people who populated the bar raised their calculators and toasted the generosity of their new-found friend. Then out came the work, load after load after load after load after load, until Rev. Van Winkle's brain was spinning and leaping and twirling and dancing.

To this workaholic minister, the world had begun to revolve at blurry-brained speeds. Rev. Van Winkle tried to get up from his stool, but it was like trying to step from a moving carnival ride. He was flung against the floor, with pieces of his mind crashing in on all sides.

When the pandemonium subsided and the earth returned to its steady spin, Rev. Van Winkle felt a small dose of adrenalin still throwing itself around in his system, as if it were trying to recapture the crazy motion of before.

Rev. Van Winkle stood up and, as he did, his legs cracked with stiffness. "I must've sat on that barstool too long," he said, brushing a thick layer of dust from his pants.

Finally regaining sense enough to gaze at his surroundings, Rev. Van Winkle was shocked. The inside of the workaholic bar was now vacant and rotted. Cobwebs, which occupied every portion of the room, billowed like the sails of a ship.

"What in the world?" Rev. Van Winkle said aloud. As he spoke, his voice barely worked its way out of his dry, gummed-up throat. Coughing uncontrollably, he stumbled through the rubble and into the brightness of day.

Block after block presented only run-down buildings. But up ahead there was a group of glass buildings like nothing he had ever seen before—except in movies by George Lucas and Steven Spielberg. They were downright extraterrestrial.

"This must be a dream," Rev. Van Winkle muttered again and again until he found himself standing at the very spot once occupied by his old church. In its place was a new, futuristic church.

As a service began to let out, Rev. Van Winkle slowly ascended the stairs, entered the church, and stared at the sci-fi clothing of the churchgoers. They returned the stare, for his clothes were faded and moldy. Even his clerical collar had become gray with age.

"Who are you people?" he finally shouted, bringing a group of men to a halt. "And what are you doing at my church?" he added, after noting that this building still carried the name of his old congregation.

"Should we call the police?" whispered a fellow.

"My name is Rev. Van Winkle!" the old minister declared. "Doesn't anyone here know me?"

"I think we should call the police," repeated the whisper.

"You *must* know me. I am the pastor of this church!"

The deacons of the congregation were about to escort Rev. Van Winkle from the sanctuary when a woman carrying a baby walked forward out of the crowd. She stepped before the bearded man in the moldy clothes and inspected him intensely.

"Is that you, Father?" she exclaimed.

Rev. Van Winkle gasped. "Donna?"

The woman stepped back, as if physically pushed. "It's true. It *is* my father!"

As murmurs of disbelief passed through the crowd, Rev. Van Winkle moved closer to his daughter. "But Donna, how did you grow so quickly! I'm so . . . so . . ."

"If you had spent any time with your family, maybe you wouldn't be surprised to see me grown," Donna said sharply. "I haven't seen you for twenty years."

Rev. Van Winkle slowly lowered himself onto a pew. It was overwhelming. "And your mother. My wife. How is my wife?"

"She's been dead for twelve years, Father."

"Dead? But why didn't she tell me?"

"She phoned you from her deathbed, but your secretary was screening your calls."

"I can't believe this," Rev. Van Winkle muttered. "And what about my son? What became of Lawrence?"

"We never see him anymore because he inherited your craving for work. He even loves to quote your favorite expression: 'On the seventh day, God rested, and He felt guilty about it.' "

"Will you ever forgive me?" Rev. Van Winkle said, taking his daughter's hand and holding it to his face to dab away his tears.

"It will be hard to forget," Donna said. "It will be hard to forget how you always insisted on reading me bedtime paperwork instead of bedtime stories. And it will be hard to forget what Mom had to do to get your attention." According to Donna, her mom would sign an assumed name on the visitors' card at church, then put on a disguise and rent out a house for a day. That way, she could chat with her husband when he came around to make pastoral calls to visitors.

"I'm sorry," Rev. Van Winkle sobbed. "I'll make it up to you. I really will."

During the next few months, the congregation progressively became convinced that Rev. Van Winkle's strange tale was true. He *had* missed twenty years of life because of his obsessive passion for work. And as a consequence, Rev. Van Winkle became the champion of relaxation. He devoted himself to spreading the message of Sabbath rest by telling people that although the idle mind may be the devil's workshop, the workaholic mind was the devil's dining room.

With a slogan for every person he spoke with, Rev. Van Winkle became an immediate hit on the Christian speakers' circuit. He wrote a best-seller every six months and he started his own magazine, as well as a local chapter of Workaholics Anonymous. Television appearances and product endorsements were next, followed by his own radio show aimed at couples that had been broken apart by a workaholic spouse. He called the show *Focus on What's Left of Your Family*.

As part of his weekly routine, Rev. Van Winkle would appear at two luncheons; run three small groups; answer a deluge of mail; take phone calls at every hour of the night; host his new radio show; write three magazine articles; meet with local, state, and national politicians; and chair a committee on National Workaholic Awareness Week.

On Tuesdays, his schedule was even busier.

PART FOUR

Blessed are those who hunger and thirst for righteousness, for they will be filled.

10

LIFE IS THE CHILDHOOD OF OUR IMMORTALITY.
(Johann Wolfgang Von Goethe)

A friend named Ann once told of her first year as a Christian. She was fired up for Christ, she had enthusiasm rocketing from under her feet, and she *had* to tell somebody about it.

"Don't worry," Ann's minister said after she described her new-found enthusiasm for the Lord. "You'll get over it."

Unbelievable. A new Christian on fire for God comes to a minister and he promptly douses her with a bucket of cynical water. Ann later conjectured that maybe the minister had seen his share of new Christians sputter out. Maybe the minister assumed she was just another quick-to-fizzle Christian. But, as Ann went on to say, the minister still had no excuse for his attitude.

In the following story, we witness another demonstration of this hunger for God, this thirst for life. And we witness another demonstration of pessimism at its worst. The story is based on the work of Dr. Mortimer Klondike, a surgeon who recently stunned the scientific community. For the first time, he recorded a conversation between unborn twins who were waiting to be delivered into the world. One baby hungered for new life and the other was a prenatal cynic.

Some scientists do not believe this recording is authentic, mainly because Dr. Klondike could not stop from giggling when he announced his accomplishment at a press conference. Nevertheless, in the interest of science I am proud to present the conversation that Dr. Klondike claims took place between twins who were later named Boregarde and Sharon.

MATERNITY
SHARON
BOREGARDE

BABY TALK

SHARON: Wow! Look at that! I never imagined preparing for birth could be so exciting.

BOREGARDE: I never imagined preparing for birth could be so noisy. Will you be quiet?

SHARON: How can you sleep when there's so much happening?

BOREGARDE: How can I sleep when you won't shut up?

SHARON: I talk a lot when I get excited.

BOREGARDE: You call this exciting? We've been sitting in this tiny place for nine months. The least they could have done was leave us a few magazines to read.

SHARON: Look at that! And look at *that* over there!

BOREGARDE: *Please* be quiet. I asked for a private womb, and what did I get? A blabber-mouth wombmate.

SHARON: Can I ask you just one question?

BOREGARDE: No.

SHARON: What do you think it'll be like after we're born?

BOREGARDE: If you really want to know, I don't believe *anything* happens after we're born. We just disappear from the face of the earth.

SHARON: You don't believe in life after birth?

BOREGARDE: Absolutely not. That's just a myth babies invented so they wouldn't be afraid of being born.

SHARON: A myth?

BOREGARDE: That's right. Listen, Sis, what makes you think that anything exists outside this little dark room of ours?

SHARON: What about those voices I keep hearing out there? Why, just yesterday I heard a woman say, "I can't wait till these twins are born so I can swim without my stomach hitting the bottom of the pool."

BOREGARDE: That's just your imagination. Delusions, they call them.

SHARON: I think it's M*om's* voice. Who else could it be?

BOREGARDE: Sorry, Sis, but I don't believe in the existence of Mom.

SHARON: What? I suppose you don't believe that Dad exists either!

BOREGARDE: Of course not. No intelligent person believes in Dad anymore.

SHARON: But if Dad doesn't exist, then who keeps saying, "It's crazy to attend so many prenatal classes when we're not even planning to give birth to a natal?"

BOREGARDE: I told you. It's your imagination.

SHARON: But who created us if it wasn't Mom and Dad?

BOREGARDE: I don't know, and I really don't care. Now let me sleep.

SHARON: But if you don't believe anything exists after birth, aren't you scared about being born?

BOREGARDE: (Pause) Well . . . I guess I'm sort of scared. That's why I decided that I'm *not* going to be born.

SHARON: And miss out on everything in life?

BOREGARDE: "Everything" doesn't exist. Myths. Just myths.

SHARON: How can you say that, Boregarde?

BOREGARDE: Boregarde?

SHARON: That's what I heard Mom say she might name you.

BOREGARDE: Then I'm *definitely* not going to be born.

SHARON: If you ask me, you're going to have a pretty dull existence if you stay in this dark, wet little place when you could . . . Look! There's a light.

BOREGARDE: Big deal. You've seen one light, you've seen them all.

SHARON: Boregarde, I think this is it! Hang on to your hat, we're about to be born.

BOREGARDE: You're crazy. Life after birth is just an invention to sooth our primitive egos. It's just a wish fulfillment that . . .

SHARON: I hope I look all right for Mom and Dad. Is my hair okay?

BOREGARDE: You don't have any hair.

SHARON: Then is my scalp okay? Look! I think I caught a glimpse of a doctor. This is really *it*.

BOREGARDE: There's no such thing as a doctor.

SHARON: I'm nervous. What am I going to say to Mom and Dad? I want to make a good impression. Maybe I should say, "Hi Mom. Hi Dad. I know you've put up with a lot the last nine months, so I decided that for the next two years I'll change my own diapers."

BOREGARDE: Will you get your foot out of my face?

SHARON: Sorry. I guess I'm too excited. Hi Dad! Maybe if I wave, he'll see me. I feel like a butterfly about to burst from a cocoon. What do you feel like?

BOREGARDE: More like a hardened criminal, hiding from the law. I can hear the news report now: "Boregarde Perkins, alias 'Babyface' Perkins, is still unwilling to be born and is reportedly at large—ten pounds, two ounces to be exact. He stands twenty-two inches tall, has no teeth, and should be approached with caution because he has been known to drool on people without the slightest provocation. Babyface is—"

SHARON: Here we go, Brother Boy. Geronimo!

BOREGARDE: This is ridiculous. Absolutely ridiculous. There's no such thing as life after birth. There's no such thing as Mom and Dad and doctors and . . .

Dr. Klondike's recording of the twins ended at this point, but one of the nurses fortunately kept a record of the birth:

"I helped deliver twins today. The boy was a real troublesome sort. He came out kicking and screaming, his eyes closed and his arms flailing. When he finally opened his eyes, he seemed shocked. And when we wheeled him to the nursery, he had a baffled, almost angry expression of disbelief on his face. Probably just gas.

"As for the baby girl, she was another story. She came into the world all smiles, almost as if she thought the experience was an obstetrical amusement-park ride.

"In fact, given the chance, I wouldn't be surprised if the baby girl would do it all over, just so she could revel in the thrill of being born again."

11

MORE THAN ANY OTHER TIME IN HISTORY, MANKIND FACES A CROSSROADS. ONE PATH LEADS TO DESPAIR AND UTTER HOPELESSNESS. THE OTHER, TO TOTAL EXTINCTION. LET US PRAY WE HAVE THE WISDOM TO CHOOSE CORRECTLY.

(Woody Allen)

The search for meaning in life is a universal quest. This theme recurs again and again in the work of comedian Woody Allen, who focuses on (some say he is obsessed with) the despair of modern life.

For example, writing about the decay of society in *Side Effects*, Allen says that "by 1990 kidnapping will be the dominant mode of social interaction. Overpopulation will exacerbate problems to the breaking point. Figures tell us there are already more people on earth than we need to move even the heaviest piano. If we do not call a halt to breeding, by the year 2000 there will be no room to serve dinner unless one is willing to set the table on the heads of strangers. . . . Of course energy will be in short supply and each car owner will be allowed only enough gasoline to back up a few inches."

The despair of modern humanity is understandable when we consider the meaningless things people use to quench their thirst for meaning. But, fortunately, there really *is* a way to find meaning. Let us follow the steps of a person trying to find it.

THE MYSTERY OF LIFE MYSTERY

I was finally on to something big. Really big. I rushed to a phone booth and called up the boss.

"Mr. Z," I said. "This is Mick. I got a lead. . . . That's right. . . . I think I narrowed it down to one suspect. . . . Yes, I got his apartment staked out now. . . . He isn't going anywhere without me on his tail. Gotta go. The light just went out in his apartment."

For three years, I had been working on this case—trying to locate the meaning of life. People have been searching for the meaning of life for thousands of years, so this was no task for a rookie. That's why they hired me—Mick Anvil, private eye.

I slipped into the shadows and waited for my suspect to appear. I was sure this guy would lead me to the meaning of life. Three years of work was reaching a climax.

A door creaked open, and I heard the suspect's footsteps. I peeked around the corner and spotted the suspect slipping into the back seat of a taxi. I had to act fast, or I'd lose him in the afternoon traffic jam.

Hailing the next taxi, I leaped into the front seat. "Follow that car!" I shouted.

"Righto," said the driver, and the taxi squealed off.

Then I realized the taxi had another passenger—an old man in the back seat. He tapped me on the shoulder. "Excuse me," he said, "but I think I can—"

The taxi ahead of us slammed to a stop, and the suspect

jumped out and rushed toward a high-rise building—the headquarters for Mega-Power Unlimited, Incorporated, and Company.

Before you could say "Columbo's wife," I was out of the taxi and in hot pursuit. This is it, I thought. The suspect was leading me where I had hoped—right to the meaning of life.

The suspect headed into the headquarters for the richest, most powerful corporation in the world. It made perfect sense. Surely the people who directed this storehouse of power and wealth would know the meaning of life.

Inside the high-rise, I flashed my badge at a security guard and bounded upstairs. Then I turned the corner just in time to see the suspect slip into an office. I was close. Inside that office, I would find the meaning of life.

Kicking in the door and leaping into the room, I shouted, "Freeze! Police!" But then I stopped, shocked. The inside of the office looked like a decaying old shack. Walls had crumbled, and rats were nibbling at the frayed carpet. I wouldn't find the meaning of life there.

"I was trying to tell you about this," said a voice from behind. I spun around and saw the old man from the taxi. "The meaning of life cannot be found in wealth and property," he said. "Wealth fades, property decays, and power is fleeting. It is all vanity and striving after wind."

He was right. This wasn't the place. I glanced out the window just in time to see the suspect back on street level and climbing into his taxi. Before you could say "James Bond," I shot down the staircase, into my taxi, and shouted, "Follow that car!"

I didn't know how I'd let the suspect slip through my fingers, but I wasn't going to let it happen again. Nobody does that twice to Mick Anvil.

To my surprise, the pesky old man was in the back seat again, leaning on his cane.

"Aha!" I exclaimed, sticking my head out the window. "There he is!"

Having spotted the suspect's taxi, we were back on the

trail. And wouldn't you know it; the suspect's taxi was headed into the heart of the university.

I should have realized it from the start. Where else would the meaning of life be found except in the halls of higher learning?

"Excuse me," said the old man, tapping me on the shoulder. "But I think you ought—"

"No time, old man!" I leaped from the car while it was still in motion, and before you could say "Kojak," I was racing through the dark halls of the philosophy building.

"Did you see a big man in a gray suit go by?" I asked a student, and he pointed to a spiral staircase that led to an ivory tower.

Up, up, and up the stairs I rushed. At the top of the landing, I threw my weight against a heavy oak door and somersaulted into a room. But what I found was *not* the meaning of life. Several philosophy professors were huddled in a corner, weeping as if they were at a funeral.

"I tried to tell you," said the old man, appearing at my side again. "Wisdom can be fine and good. But without God, wisdom just opens our eyes to the pain of life without offering any hope. It increases pain. Vanity of vanities. All is vanity."

I was furious. The suspect had given me the slip again, and it was night before I could catch up with him. When I spotted him, he was in disguise and entering the Pleasure Dome—the palace of earthly delight where people go to tingle their senses and feed their desires.

The Pleasure Dome *had* to hold the key. It was an island of gluttonous fun that protected people from suffering. Surely I would find the meaning of life there.

"This is a raid!" I shouted, bursting into the building, waving my revolver. Then I snapped at the owner: "The game is up. I know you have the meaning of life hidden in the back room."

On my command, one of the Pleasure Dome employees hesitantly reached for the key to the back room. I was ready to find what I was after.

But what was this? When the employee opened the door, I stood staring into an empty room.

"Vanity of vanities." Once again I heard that annoying voice of the old man. This time he stormed into the Pleasure Dome, overturning tables and smashing bottles of mind-mummifying drugs. "Pleasure apart from God is empty! Meaningless! Remember your Creator in the days of your youth, before the sun, the moon, and the stars are darkened!"

Remember the Creator? That old man must have known more than I thought. I followed him as he walked outside, and I shouted after him, "Hey you!" The old man turned to face me. "Do *you* know where I can find the meaning of life?"

The old man just smiled, turned away, and walked into the thickening mist. I tried to track him down, but he had completely vanished—except for a black book that he had dropped on the pavement. It was probably his manual for breaking codes.

Flipping to the first page, I began to read: "In the beginning God created the heavens and the earth. . . ."

As I read on, my eyes widened and I whistled. "This is it."

Trembling, I slid the book into my coat pocket, pulled my coat collar up around my neck, and vanished into the fog.

12

"WITHOUT CHILDREN I WOULD BE COMFORTABLE WITH $200,000 A YEAR. MONEY MEANS A LOT TO MY HAPPINESS. I WANT TO BE ABLE TO GO TO EUROPE WHEN I WANT TO, TO BUY CLOTHES WHEN I WANT TO."

(A 28-year-old)

Yuppies, or Young Urban Professionals, deserve mention because they symbolize everything the Beatitudes warn us against. Rather than thirsting and hungering after righteousness, Yuppies thirst and hunger after money, power, and professional prestige.

But I'm not telling you anything new. In fact, is there anything new to say about Yuppies?

Yes, there is. I would like to be the first to mention the latest danger—a danger posed by "Yurpies," or Young R*ural* Professionals. It's true. The Yuppie mentality has even invaded the farm. And we've got trouble, my friends. Right here in River City. Therefore, I suggest that you be on the lookout for these tell-tale signs of agricultural Yuppiness.

Is the farmer down the road irrigating his crops with Perrier? Is your neighbor's hired hand dressing his pigs in striped leotards and making them burn off calories in a Jane Fonda exercise class? Has Farmer Jones stopped growing corn and planted 500 acres of pasta instead? Does his tractor have a ceiling fan in it?

Remember, you heard it here first. The Yuppie philosophy is moving into the heartland, and it is sure to cause a heartland attack.

On second thought, perhaps what I just told you is nothing new at all. The self-seeking Yuppie mentality has been with us since the beginning of time, and variations of it can be found everywhere—even on a farm in Kansas.

I wouldn't even be surprised to find a bit of the Yuppie mentality somewhere over the rainbow.

THE YUPPIE OF OZ

Dorothy stood in the middle of a Kansas wheat field, waiting for a tornado to arrive.

She was sick of Kansas. She was sick of wheat. She was sick of her family's life in the country. And she was sick of their traditional beliefs, their trust in God, and their apple pie.

She craved something different and exciting. That's why she turned her thoughts to the land of Oz, the place she had visited years ago. Now *there* was a place with action.

A tornado had flung her to Oz for her first visit, so she figured that a tornado was the way to travel again. With suitcase in hand, she stood in the wheat field and stared at the approaching storm. A businessman stood next to her with a newspaper in his hands.

"You waiting for the 3 o'clock tornado?" he asked, glancing at his watch.

"You bet," said Dorothy.

"Well, I hope it isn't too crowded. It's vacation season, so the tornado will be jammed with tourists traveling to Oz."

Bearing down on them, the black, spinning twister sucked up everything in its path. It roared through the wheat field, plucked Dorothy and the businessman from the ground, and proceeded onward, twirling objects and people upward and upward until they landed somewhere over the rainbow.

Dorothy was amazed at the changes in Oz. Munchkins raced along in Mercedes-Benz automobiles, and gourmet foods were temptingly arrayed at sidewalk cafes. To put it simply, Oz had gone to the Yuppies.

Dorothy had never seen such an exciting variety of wealth and gadgetry—VCRs and computers and video cameras and microwaves galore. These were things she could trust, Dorothy decided. Things that could be seen and touched. But how could she afford them?

"Why don't you get yourself a credit card?" came a voice from behind. Wheeling around, Dorothy found herself staring at an old friend—the Scarecrow.

My, how he had changed! The Scarecrow, wearing an elaborate jogging outfit, had a computer attached to his waist to measure his heart rate and calorie loss.

"In the land of Oz, you're a nobody without possessions," he said. "And in the land of Oz, you cannot buy possessions without a credit card. Where do you get a credit card in Oz? Why, from the Yuppie of Oz, of course! And how do you find the Yuppie of Oz? At the end of the Yellow Brick Fast Lane, of course!"

The Scarecrow loaned Dorothy a pair of two-hundred-dollar running shoes and told her that he would be happy to jog with her down the Yellow Brick Fast Lane if she would enroll in his $7,500-per-year health club.

Linking arms just like in the old days, the Scarecrow and Dorothy began to jog down the crowded path. As they did, they sang a merry tune:

"We're off to see the Yuppie!
The wonderful Yuppie of Oz!
Because, because, because, BECAUSE!
Because of the money he lends us!"

They hadn't jogged more than a mile before another old friend appeared on the horizon. Good old Tin Woodman. But he was no longer into chopping trees. The Tin Woodman, now a Tin Millionaire, was very much into stocks and bonds. He owned a huge, rust-proof mansion and had a staff of fifty-six servants to keep him well-oiled.

The Yuppie of Oz

The Tin Millionaire attended the Church of the Almighty Buck where they worshiped money and prayed, "Our dollar, which art invested, hallowed be thy capital gains. Thy dividends come. Thy compounding be done, in stocks as it is in bonds. Give us this day our daily interest, and forgive us our debts, but not our debtors. And lead us not into recession, but deliver us from double-digit inflation. For thine is the kingdom, and the power, and the glory, for now. Amen."

The Tin Millionaire said he would simply *love* to jog down the Yellow Brick Fast Lane with his old friends, Scarecrow and Dorothy. He clipped a cordless phone to his belt, slipped on a pair of tin Adidas shoes, and off they went.

If only Aunt Em could see her now, Dorothy thought. Here she was, racing down the Yellow Brick Fast Lane in expensive jogging shoes. And she would soon have her own credit card to buy things that Aunt Em could never even imagine—a posh apartment on the lake, a Jaguar, fine clothes . . .

These delightful thoughts were temporarily interrupted when a lion came bounding from the doorway of a nearby restaurant and threw his arms around Dorothy. Then he stepped back and gave out a mighty roar: "I AM KING OF THE GOURMETS!"

It was another old friend—the Cowardly Lion. But as Dorothy discovered, the Cowardly Lion was not too cowardly when it came to experimenting with exotic food. No simple apple pie for him. According to the lion, the only meal worth eating was one that couldn't be pronounced easily and cost at least $56.

The Cowardly Lion, whose cooking ability was well-known in Oz, had been renamed "the Gourmet Lion." He was even a regular guest on "Lifestyles of the Rich and Carnivorous."

"We're off to see the Yuppie of Oz!" said the Scarecrow.

"Oh, that sounds wonderful!" roared the Gourmet Lion, hopping on his $4,000 bicycle to join the fun.

"We're off to see the Yuppie!
The wonderful Yuppie of Oz!

Because, because, because, BECAUSE!
Because of the money he lends us!"

Emerald City, home of the Yuppie of Oz, was more than Dorothy imagined. She had never seen so many limousines and health spas all in one spot.

These were things she could see. These were things she could trust.

"And what brings you before the great and mighty Oz!" came the voice from above when Dorothy, the Scarecrow, the Tin Millionaire, and the Gourmet Lion entered into the presence of the Almighty Yuppie himself.

Up front was a huge, youthful face with a sweat band across its forehead. The face filled an entire wall. It was the great Oz.

"Please sir," Dorothy said, bowing, "I'd like a credit card. I'd like to dress for success. I'd like to grab for all the gusto I can get. Because . . . because I deserve it, sir."

The mighty Oz was about to ask whether she had any marketable skills when the door at the back of the room edged open and a tiny dog came pattering across the marble floor. It was Toto, Dorothy's faithful friend who had followed her from Kansas.

A look of panic appeared on the huge face of Oz as Toto trotted over to a curtain at the back of the room. Toto gripped the curtain in his teeth and swung it open. Behind the curtain, a bald-headed little man, hunched over by age, was busily working the gears that controlled the huge face on the wall.

Aghast, the Scarecrow exclaimed, "Why, you're not one of the young and beautiful people! You're a phony!"

The Yuppie of Oz hobbled out of his booth. He paused in front of Dorothy, looked down at his feet for the longest time, and then sighed. "He's right, my dear. I'm just a small person who's afraid of growing old. Our society doesn't have much tolerance for people with wrinkles. So I pretended to be a Yuppie—a young, rich go-getter."

Shocked and very confused, Dorothy sobbed, "But can't I still get a credit card? I came here to buy lots of things! What's so bad about good food and nice stereos and—"

"There's nothing bad about things, as long as you don't love them," said Oz. "Take it from me. I know from experience that material things can't be trusted; they just don't last. Observe."

With these words, the great Oz picked up a bucket of water and tossed it on the Scarecrow, the Gourmet Lion, and the Tin Millionaire. As the water made contact, the Scarecrow's portable computer, the Gourmet Lion's $4,000 bicycle, and the Tin Millionaire's cordless telephone all dissolved into steam and bubbles—just like wicked witches melting into the ground.

As they wiped the water from their eyes, Dorothy's friends smiled. They were finally free from their possessions.

For the first time, the Scarecrow could use his brain for something other than comparison shopping. The Gourmet Lion could stop worrying about whether he impressed people. And the Tin Millionaire could put his heart into helping others with his money instead of always helping himself.

After bidding farewell to their friends, Dorothy and Toto took the six o'clock tornado back to Kansas. They enjoyed dinner in-flight and arrived home just as Aunt Em was putting an apple pie on the table. Dorothy didn't even mind that her suitcase, which contained all of her possessions, had been sent to Cleveland by mistake.

After all, she was home.

PART FIVE

Blessed are the merciful, for they will be shown mercy.

13

TO PLAY THIS GAME YOU MUST HAVE THAT FIRE IN YOU, AND NOTHING STOKES THAT FIRE LIKE HATE.

(Vince Lombardi, former
Green Bay Packers coach)

It must be hard for Christian athletes to reconcile the spirit of mercy with the spirit of competition.

In basketball, if somebody steals the ball, do you give him your shirt and warm-up jacket as well? In football, should you tackle the opposition by using diplomacy and passive resistance? If you tried to reason with fullbacks, could you convince them of the benefits of voluntarily falling to the Astroturf?

As I see it, the only way to get football players to be more peaceful is to get them to approve the unilateral disarmament of middle linebackers over 250 pounds. And the only way to get them to do that is to make them think they are supporting the concept of unilateral *dismemberment*.

To be truthful, though, I'm not really as concerned about how to apply Christian mercy to sports as I am about how to *avoid* applying the merciless, win-at-any-cost, sports ethic to Christianity. To some people, faith is nothing but another contest, a trophy for the den.

Consider the example of Macey, son of the Mighty Casey.

I Never Promised You a Hot Tub

THE THIRD STRIKE

Somewhere you've probably heard the immortal tale of Mighty Casey—a tale that ended like this:

Oh, somewhere in this favored land
The sun is shining bright,
The band is playing somewhere,
And somewhere hearts are light;
And somewhere men are laughing,
And somewhere children shout,
But there is no joy in Mudville;
Mighty Casey has struck out.

That story was told over eighty years ago, so you might be wondering what ever happened to Mighty Casey after that fateful day when he struck out with two outs and the tying run in scoring position.

Good question.

To find out what happened to Casey, I recently hired the services of noted sports analyst Archibald Avery. (As you probably know, Avery was the first one to theorize that it would be too obvious if a third-base coach gave a "steal sign" by sticking his foot behind his head while singing "Take Me Out to the Ball Game" in Chinese.)

After approximately twenty seconds of in-depth research, Avery compiled a 4,500-page report on Mighty Casey. I have the fullest confidence that much of this information is accurate, particularly the last two words of the third sentence in the first paragraph.

In his report, Avery disclosed that Mighty Casey had been

shunned by Mudville residents immediately following his disastrous strike-out. Casey's family seriously considered trading him in for a new car, and everyone in town gave him the silent treatment for twelve years—behavior that greatly improved the town's skill at charades.

Casey was a loser, people said, and nobody wanted to associate with a loser.

But, lo and behold, Casey eventually was greeted with an amazing twist of fortune. His wife gave birth to a boy who appeared to be a born winner. The baby boy, Macey, was clearly endowed with a natural love and talent for sports.

In fact, according to the nurse who assisted with the birth, Casey's son was the first baby she saw who was born with the word *Nike* imprinted on the back of his heels.

Casey was ecstatic. Since he had been a flop in sports, he hoped with all his might that Macey would once again bring athletic glory to their family name.

At first, Casey's hopes seemed to be realized. Macey was such a sports fanatic that he insisted his diapers have Adidas stripes, and at every meal he donned a catcher's chest protector instead of a bib. He even asked for a stopwatch on his six-month birthday, just so he could time his mom and dad in freestyle diaper-changing competition.

As the years progressed, though, Casey's excitement over Macey's athletic eagerness transformed into annoyance and then a deep dread. Something was terribly wrong with Macey.

To Macey, *everything* was a contest. For instance, at age two he installed a scoreboard in his bedroom so he could keep track of who was ahead whenever his brother and sister argued with each other.

At age five, he began to release a weekly AP ranking of friends, in the order of preference. And at the end of the year, he chose an all-star team of friends and awarded an MVP trophy to his closest friend for the year.

At age seven, Macey began to look at everything in terms of statistics. He even devised a complicated system for figuring his mom's EKA, or Earned Kiss Average. At age ten, he became a school bully and kept tally of the number of kids he beat up; RBIs he called them, or "runts batted in."

So the next question in your mind is probably this: What eventually became of Casey and his egomaniac, sports fanatic son?

Good question.

For an answer, I once again consulted sports analyst Archibald Avery, who was working at the time on a book about the best way to transport a pole vault in a crowded elevator. After twelve seconds of intensive research on our question, Avery uncovered the following exclusive poem, which recounts the fate of Mighty Casey's mighty obnoxious son:

MIGHTY MACEY, SON OF CASEY

Casey, Mighty Casey, was known for striking out.
His slugging days were over. He lost his famous
clout.
Sympathy was lacking in every fan he saw,
And those who once applauded, now scorned his
every flaw.

But Casey had a son, whose middle name was
Sports.
And his first name? It was Macey—a superstar of
sorts.
Macey won at golf and track. He won at baseball
too.
He won at football every year. His ego grew and
grew.

I Never Promised You a Hot Tub

Sports was Macey's idol, and come one Christmas day,
He gave his mom some high-heeled cleats. She knew not what to say.
Macey also had three brothers, all born out near Detroit.
But what he called them was quite odd—Spalding, Rawlings, and young Voit.

In the quarterback position, Mighty Macey had no peer.
And when Macey took the pitcher's mound, each batter hid in fear.
When Macey tried out golf one day, he smacked a hole in one.
And in track that year, his discus throw went somewhere near the sun.

In Olympic competition, Mighty Macey forged ahead.
He won twelve golds and, sure as fire, his pride was quite well fed.
Then at the age of twenty-one, Macey made his fateful choice.
"In baseball I am going pro, so fans you may rejoice!"

He was paid a million bucks per year—that is, one thousand Gs.
And with dough like that, he told his dad, "I'll do as I well please."
He bought up everything in sight, and paid for every thrill.
He even used his cash as fuel to start his charcoal grill.

The Third Strike

A film about his rise to fame was Macey's next desire.
And sure enough it came to pass with *Limousines of Fire.*
In the film, we see him run and run along the sand,
As advertisers sprint behind and shout, "Help sell our brand!"

Then one day, somewhere near noon, his father came to say
That Macey had become too proud; it's time he learned to pray.
But Macey spoke with angry words: "Get out! Don't spoil my fun!"
So his father sadly left the room and said, "There goes strike one."

Four years went by and Macey's greed just grew and grew and grew,
Until a stranger came along to tell him what was true.
"I'm an angel out of heaven," said this stranger with a gleam.
But Macey muttered, "Angels? You mean that California team?"

The angel told him, "God would like repentance from you now.
Just say you need His gift of love. Just make this solemn vow."
But Macey said, "I've *earned* God's love. I *won* His love, it's true!"
So the angel shrugged and walked away and muttered, "There's strike two."

I Never Promised You a Hot Tub

The years raced by and Macey's fame had spread
across the earth.
But time was short for it had been a century since
his birth.
And as his final hours came, a voice both loud and
bold
Said, "Macey, this is God, you know, a power to
behold!"

God said His love is given free, but even better
still
It isn't won by poise or luck. It isn't earned by
skill.
Macey was outraged at this and said, "If I were
you,
My love would be a hard-earned prize awarded to
a few!

"In fact," he said, "if I were God, I wouldn't think
so small.
I'd have a *contest* for my love. The winner takes it
all!"
As Macey blabbed, he failed to see his life and
soul descend.
He didn't notice time was up. His days were soon
to end.

Oh, somewhere in this favored land, the sun is
shining bright,
The band is playing somewhere, and somewhere
hearts are light.
And somewhere men are laughing; and somewhere
children shout.
But there was only shock in Macey's eyes when he
learned he had struck out.

14

A MAN THAT STUDIETH REVENGE KEEPS HIS OWN WOUNDS GREEN WHICH OTHERWISE WOULD HEAL AND DO WELL.
(Francis Bacon)

In 1958, a six-year-old black girl named Ruby Bridges was ushered from a New Orleans grade school and greeted by a screaming mob. Angry people pressed in around her, shaking fists and threatening her with death.

She was the first black to attend that school.

If I had been she, I would have been fantasizing the destruction of every one of those racists. As *Time* magazine essayist Lance Morrow wrote, "Such scenes open a little trap door at the base of the brain. From that ancient root cellar they summon up dark, flapping fantasies of revenge."

Humans have a long history of vengeance. Morrow noted that in one culture, women have their infants sleep on the bloody shirts of their murdered husbands. From infancy, these children are brought up in an atmosphere of vengeance.

In our society we don't lay babies on blood-stained shirts, but we have other ways to raise our children to avenge. We present them with "heroes" like Rambo or Dirty Harry.

In contrast, Jesus tossed aside such notions with the simple words, "Blessed are the merciful."

And then there is Ruby Bridges. What did she do in the face of hatred? She prayed for those who persecuted her.

The psychologists from Harvard were astounded.

DICK AND JANE GET A LESSON IN THEOLOGY

See Dick. See Jane. See Spot. Dick and Jane are Christians. But Spot is not. He is a collie.

See Dick read the Bible. Read, read, read. The Bible says that God is merciful. He forgives all of our sins, and this makes Dick glad. "If God forgives all of my sins, that means I can sin all I want and not worry," he says.

"That is bad theology," says Jane.

Spot barks. "Bark, bark, bark!" He does not like Dick's theology either. Spot should know. He reads C. S. Lewis.

But that does not matter to Dick. He likes to sin. And God will forgive all of his sins. Right?

See Dick sin. Sin, sin, sin. He likes to get mad, and he is merciless to people. Especially to Jeremy Hess. Dick likes to turn red in the face and shout at Jeremy. Red is a pretty color. Do you like the colòr red?

"You should not hate Jeremy," says Jane. "You must love him."

See Dick stuff a rag in Jane's mouth. Ugh. Dick does not care if he is sinning or not. He is forgiven. He is free.

During lunchtime at work, Dick likes to eat. And eat. And eat. And eat. Dick is a glutton. See Dick carry his lunch bag in a forklift. It is a large bag.

See Dick eat his lunch. See Dick eat Jeremy's lunch. See Dick eat twenty-one sandwiches, fourteen Twinkies, four bags of potato chips, seven candy bars, and two malted milks. His co-workers are impressed. He can really snarf it down.

"You must not eat so much," says Jane. "People in other parts of the world are hungry. Jeremy is hungry."

Dick and Jane Get a Lesson in Theology

See Dick laugh at Jane. See Dick lock Jane in a filing cabinet and then leave work. "Bark, bark, bark!" says Spot. In dog language this means, "Did you lock Jane in a filing cabinet again?"

But Dick does not care what happens to Jane. And he does not care if he is merciless. He is forgiven for his sins. He is free.

Dick has a different sin for every day of the week. On Sundays he gossips. On Mondays he cheats. On Tuesdays he lies. On Wednesdays he steals. On Thursdays he is greedy. On Fridays he harasses Jeremy Hess. On Saturdays he is cruel to animals.

Spot leaves the country every Saturday.

But Dick does not worry. He is forgiven. He is free.

One morning there is a knock at the home of Dick and Jane. An official-looking man is at the door.

"You must come with me," says the man to Dick. "You have been made a slave. You are our property. We are going to put you up for sale today."

See Dick try to close the door. See the man stick his foot in the door and grab Dick by the collar.

"I am not a slave," says Dick. "There is a mistake here."

"You are a slave to sin," says the man. "You are *our* slave. And we are going to sell you at an auction today."

See Dick cry for help. But Jane cannot hear his shouts. She is still at work, locked in a filing cabinet. Spot cannot hear his shouts either. It is Saturday and Spot is out of the country.

See the man take Dick to an auction center. Dick is in chains. "How much do I hear for this slave to sin?" says the man to the auction crowd.

Thirty dollars. Forty dollars. Fifty dollars. Sixty dollars. The price is going up, up, up. Dick is feeling down, down, down. Who is going to buy him? What will they do to him?

Seventy dollars. Eighty dollars. Ninety dollars. One hundred dollars. Dick is sold. See him being placed in a jail cell until his new owner comes to claim him. What a rotten day. Rotten, rotten, rotten.

I Never Promised You a Hot Tub

Suddenly, the door opens. Is it the new owner? Will he be mean? Will he let Dick eat Twinkies and malts for lunch? Will he provide a forklift for Dick's lunch bags? Will he . . . ?

"Uh-oh," Dick says. It is worse than he thought. His new owner is Jeremy Hess.

See Jeremy enter the room smiling. See Jeremy open the jail cell door. Will Jeremy take out his revenge? Will Jeremy lock Dick in a filing cabinet for the rest of his life?

"You are free," says Jeremy.

See Dick clear out his ears. See Dick ask Jeremy to repeat what he just said.

"You are free," says Jeremy.

"But I was merciless to you," says Dick. "Why pay to set me free?"

"Jesus paid a heavy price," says Jeremy. "And people were merciless to Him."

That is an understatement. Understatement, understatement, understatement.

"You are worth the price," says Jeremy. "You are free."

See Dick leave the cell. See Dick and Jeremy go to work and let Jane out of the filing cabinet. It was hard to find her. She was misfiled. See Dick begin to change his ways.

Dick is happy. Jane is happy. God is happy.

"Bark, bark, bark!" says Spot. He is happy too. He does not have to leave the country on Saturdays anymore.

15

MERCY IMITATES GOD, AND DISAPPOINTS SATAN. (Saint John Chrysostom)

In a 1985 issue of *Christianity Today*, a minister was quoted as saying that he felt as if he were bleeding to death. He was the fifth pastor in eight years at this particular church and now he knew why. His church was looking for someone who could please all of the people all of the time.

As the article goes on to note, we often expect pastors to excel as a servant-shepherd, prophet-politician, preacher-enthraller, teacher-theologian, evangelist-exhorter, organizer-promoter, caller-comforter, counselor-reconciler, and equipper-enabler.

It also helps if the pastor can part the water in the baptismal.

When it comes to our pastors, why can't we show more mercy? Why do we demand so much? Pastor Tut would like to know. He is the pastor who would be king.

THE PASTOR WHO WOULD BE KING

When the tomb of the Egyptian boy-king, Tutankhamen, was uncovered in 1922, it attracted worldwide attention, not to mention a lot of flies. However, King Tut's third cousin, fifteen times removed by palace guards, is beginning to receive the attention he never deserved. His name: Rev. Tut, the boy preacher.

Three years ago, the Institute for Very Old and Dusty Things authorized an archaeology and gravity-free shuffleboard team to travel to the Valley of Preachers in Wheaton, Illinois. The Institute took an enormous risk by hiring a virtual unknown to lead the archaeological team. His name was Virgil Zich, and his only previous accomplishment had been a dig in which he uncovered fourteen cents in loose change, three pencils, five Life Savers, and a petrified piece of potato salad from underneath the cushions of a neighbor's couch.

But the choice paid off. The team eventually unearthed a golden church bus containing the mummy of Rev. Tut, a preacher who reigned in ancient Egypt. According to preliminary reports, the boy preacher was well-preserved, despite a bad case of dragon mouth that overwhelmed fifteen laborers and dissolved two stone pillars at the nearby Billy Graham Center.

Based on the relics thus far uncovered from the church bus, Dr. Zich has been able to piece together some of the circumstances surrounding the strange life of Rev. Tut.

From the very beginning the boy preacher had problems, for he feared that his family didn't love him. Perhaps this was because his father—a retired earlobe chiropractor—ordered an artist to alter the family portrait by painting a black rectangle across the eyes of Rev. Tut. Or perhaps Rev. Tut's fear of rejection started when he became distraught at the number of visitors who came to the hospital after he had his tonsils out at age seven. Hundreds of visitors came, but all of them came to see how the tonsils were doing. In fact, when it was time to be released from the hospital, the doctor asked the tonsils if they wanted to bring Rev. Tut back home in a jar.

An understanding of Rev. Tut's life would be impossible without an understanding of Egyptian culture. Ancient Egyptians had a tendency to idolize their leaders, and that is why pharaohs were considered gods. This attitude even spilled into the Egyptian church, for many believers expected their pastors to be perfect.

So, you can just imagine the problems that resulted when this most incompetent of human beings, Rev. Tut, was ordained as a minister at age fifteen and sent to Cairo to pastor a church.

It is believed that Rev. Tut reigned from two o'clock 1351 B.C. to three o'clock 1351 B.C., at which time he died of natural causes immediately following the insertion of a knife into his back. Some say he was murdered by a parishioner, while others say that he mistook his back for a stick of butter and accidentally stabbed himself. One ancient historian explained it this way:

"It is clear to *me* [italics mine] that Rev. Tut died unexpectedly. I know this for a fact because he didn't have it penciled into his *date book*." (Italics mine, but they can be yours for only $5.67. Write to: Italics, Box 1/2, Champaign, Illinois. Hurry. Limited-time offer.)

Rev. Tut was given a proper burial in a two-bedroom, unfurnished pyramid, all utilities paid. Then, after two months, he moved to a one-bedroom flat because the pharaoh above him played his stereo too loud at night. This was to be his home of eternal rest, although he also had a summer pyramid by the lake.

Actually, Rev. Tut's so-called "eternal rest" was not totally restful. Two hundred years after his death, Egyptians shifted Rev. Tut's mummy to the golden church bus in Wheaton because they wanted to turn his pyramid into a factory outlet for tie-dyed choir robes.

So there you have it—the sad tale of a pastor who just couldn't make it as a god-king for his people. Fortunately, the ancient Egyptians' concept of an infallible pastor dissolved in time, because they found that churches became unstable if they relied too heavily on one person—especially if that one person was a total nincompoop like Rev. Tut.

Besides, even if the pastor were a charismatic leader, a church's dependence spelled danger. Whenever a church was too dependent on its pastor, it often became content to sit back and let him handle the whole operation.

During the three years of digging at Wheaton, Dr. Zich uncovered a church that suffered such a fate, but few people saw the significance of the discovery—with the exception of a soused passerby who saw two significances, two Dr. Zichs, and a pink hippopotamus singing Amy Grant songs to the tune of *We Represent the Lollipop Kids*.

But other than that solitary character, few cared. Few took heed. Few even noticed as the archaeological team unburied a complete church in which 350 mummified members were sitting quietly and patiently in their pews, waiting for their pastor to put on a show.

PART SIX

Blessed are the pure in heart, for they will see God.

16

MOST PEOPLE WHO FLY FROM TEMPTATION USUALLY LEAVE A FORWARDING ADDRESS.
(Anonymous)

When Adam and Eve faced temptation in the Garden, why was it a piece of fruit? Avoiding fruit seems like a ludicrous test.

Or was it? Maybe it was the only way God could test our pure obedience to Him. In C. S. Lewis's science fiction novel *Perelandra*, a character named Ransom travels to an unfallen planet where another "Eve" is being tempted. There, he encounters this same question about God's seemingly silly tests.

Ransom responds by pointing out that much of what we call obedience to God is simply doing what makes sense to us. "Is love content with that?" Ransom says. "Where can you taste the joy of obeying unless He bids you do something for which His bidding is the *only* reason?"

Pure obedience in the face of temptation is a lofty goal. And if we expect to have even a fighting chance to maintain purity in our battles with temptation, we need a good suit of armor.

Note that I said *good* suit of armor.

I Never Promised You a Hot Tub

ARMOR FOR SALE

Morris looked the shopkeeper square in the eye. "I'd like to buy a full suit of armor to protect me from the attack of temptations."

"And what size temptations do you hope to resist?" said the shopkeeper at Ridley's Armor Shop.

"I'm expecting an extra-large one. I usually get only medium temptations. But my neighbor has been getting on my nerves lately, so I'm expecting an extra-large temptation to punch him in the nose."

"Are you interested in any particular style of armor?"

Morris pointed to the book in his hands. "This manual suggests that I put on the breastplate of righteousness. Do you have any of those?"

"No, no, no!" the shopkeeper scoffed. "Breastplates of righteousness have been out of style for years. I have something much more in vogue."

"More in vogue?" Morris said. "But isn't a breastplate of righteousness necessary to protect hearts? Doesn't it mean that when we ask God to forgive us, we have a pure heart in His eyes?"

"Where did you get that outdated manual?" said the shopkeeper, snatching the book from Morris's hands and blowing dust from its cover. "What you want is our new line of designer T-shirts."

"Designer T-shirts?"

"That's right, my friend. A breastplate of righteousness may impress God, but designer T-shirts will impress your friends. Yes sir, this T-shirt is just for you!"

Before Morris could respond, the shopkeeper handed him a T-shirt that was specially designed by the International

Fellowship of Conformists. It was emblazoned with the slogan, "I brake for peer pressure." The cash register rang like a bell; the sale was made, and the shopkeeper asked if Morris needed anything else.

"Well, if you don't think I need a breastplate of righteousness, can't you at least sell me a shield of faith to fend off temptations?" Morris said.

The shopkeeper gasped. "A shield of faith? Did I hear you correctly? My friend, do you realize how expensive a shield of faith is? Faith is a priceless item. You want something cheap and better suited to your budget, don't you?"

"Well, I don't know if—"

"I have just the thing." The shopkeeper rummaged through a desk drawer and pulled out a credit card. The card had a small handle attached to its back so that it looked like a miniature shield.

"What kind of shield is that?" Morris exclaimed.

"This is the most effective shield there is, my friend. Whenever you're tempted, simply pull out your charge card and tell Satan that you'll pay him anything if he'll just stop tempting you. Then hand him the credit card, and he'll agree to stop tempting you . . . for the time being."

Morris couldn't believe his ears. "You're suggesting that I *pay* Satan to stop tempting me? Isn't that a little bit like selling your soul to the Devil?"

"Don't worry," said the shopkeeper. "Satan takes all major credit cards."

"But I don't want to be in debt to Satan!"

"Don't worry about that either. Satan will let you make payments on the installment plan, although I admit he does have high interest rates."

Morris shook his head in confusion as the shopkeeper handed him a credit-card shield and rang up the sale.

"Next," Morris said, "my manual suggests that I wear a helmet of salvation."

According to Morris, a helmet protects one's head and

mind. When we have the assurance of salvation, he said, our minds can bask in the freedom of knowing our future is solidly with God.

"But a helmet is so confining!" said the shopkeeper. "I suggest that you not wear a helmet at all. Be a free-thinking spirit and let the breezes of the world rush through your hair."

"No helmet? But what about a sword of the Spirit? Surely, you must agree that I can't face temptation without a sword of the Spirit to cut through the confusion and help me discern right from wrong."

Again, the shopkeeper had a more fashionable suggestion. He said that swords of the Spirit are too heavy to carry around. The solution, he claimed, was to carry a small, lightweight, plastic dinner knife.

"A plastic dinner knife can't cut through anything!" Morris protested. "How can I discern right from wrong with a plastic utensil?"

"Well, my advice is not to worry about right and wrong. It's much too tiring to be concerned about."

The cash register rang again, and another sale was made.

Finally, Morris left the shop equipped from head to foot. But rather than being equipped with a breastplate of righteousness, a shield of faith, a helmet of salvation, and a sword of the Spirit, he had a T-shirt of conformity, a shield of compromise, and a sword of self-indulgence.

A few minutes later, another customer entered the shop.

"You won't believe what I just saw," the customer told the shopkeeper. "I saw a guy trying to fight off temptation with nothing but a designer T-shirt, a credit-card shield, and a plastic knife. He wasn't even wearing a helmet."

"I know," the shopkeeper smiled. "I sold him those things."

"You? Since when do *you* sell outfits for fighting temptations? I thought you were in the business of *delivering* temptations!"

"I am," the shopkeeper said. "But yesterday I put up a

sign outside saying that I was selling armor, and that fool believed it!"

After the shopkeeper and customer howled with laughter for at least a minute, the phone rang.

"Beelzebub Temptations, Inc.," the shopkeeper said into the receiver. "Yes, we do have a special deal today—two free colas with every extra-large temptation. What's that? . . . You want an extra-large temptation sent to a guy whose neighbor has been getting on his nerves? Right away. Yes, we do have free delivery . . . any time, any place."

The shopkeeper smiled a smile that could only be duplicated by a spider that had just snagged a fly in its web.

17

WITHOUT FAITH, WE ARE AS STAINED GLASS WINDOWS IN THE DARK. (Anonymous)

In his book *The Magnificent Defeat*, Frederick Buechner wondered what would happen if God rearranged the stars to spell out "I really exist."

If this action of God were the beginning to a movie, Buechner said the script would depict some people falling to their knees, some hiding in terror, and some celebrating. But the movie would end with a child calmly reading the stars and announcing to the sky, "So what if God exists? What difference does that make?"

Then the stars would fade forever from sight.

Buechner's point is that although we claim to crave physical evidence of God's existence "out there," what we really desire and what we really need to know is that God makes a difference down here in our lives.

The beauty of our Lord is that He does not spend His time (or His timelessness) just writing messages in the stars. He is active in our midst. And as the beatitude says, it takes purity of heart, not telescopes, to see Him at work. It takes faith.

THE EXPERIMENT

From the moment Sydney arrived at the house on Bloom Street, he felt like he had been sucked into a whirlwind. The door opened, and a blabbing man in a lab coat yanked him into the building.

"Welcome, welcome, welcome," the man said. "You must be the newspaper reporter who wants to find out about our scientific studies." He pulled Sydney into another room and shouted, "Hey Leonardo. The guy from the paper is here!"

A second man in a lab coat came sliding down the stairway banister and landed at Sydney's feet. "Welcome, welcome, welcome! As you probably know, we're descendants of the great inventor, Leonardo da Vinci," he said. "I'm Leonardo da Brudder . . ."

". . . and I'm Bernardo da Udder Brudder," said the other scientist. "Come. Let us show you our laboratory."

They yanked Sydney into a room cluttered with test tubes, beakers, and Bunsen burners, and Leonardo pointed at a test tube. "My friend," he said, "we are in the process of creating a vaccine to stop doubting."

He shook the green liquid in the tube. "We believe that the greatest scientific contribution we can make is to create a vaccine that will cure people of doubting the existence of God. With one injection every year, they'll know, without a doubt, that God exists."

"And to supplement the vaccine," Bernardo added, "we plan to provide indisputable, visual evidence that God exists. After all, seeing is believing. *Seeing* is believing."

Sydney opened his mouth to say something, but his words were smothered by Bernardo's jabbering.

"These are bottled prayers," Bernardo said, motioning to a row of glass jars. "To create a vaccine against doubting, we figure that we must first locate God. So, we plan to release these bottled prayers next week and track them. Our hunch is that they will lead us directly to God."

Leonardo pointed to a speedometer attached to a Bible. "And this device tells us exactly how fast the Spirit moves. According to our calculations, the Spirit moves about 435,669.9 miles per hour, unless rush-hour traffic is heavy. We figure that if we can harness the energy of the Spirit, we can use it to explode all of the doubts that run through our minds."

"Most important of all," Bernardo continued, "is faith. When people have strong faith, they are less likely to doubt. So we decided to build artificial faith out of plastic—something people can see. After all, seeing is believing."

Rushing to a closet, Leonardo pulled out a plastic shovel and chattered. "Jesus said that with enough faith we could move mountains. So we began thinking, if faith could move mountains, what would it look like?"

"And suddenly it hit us!" Bernardo shouted. "If faith can move mountains, it must look like a shovel. And this time I think we're right—not like last month when we read in the Bible about taking a 'step' of faith and thought that faith must resemble a shoe. Have you ever heard of a sillier notion than faith that looks like a shoe?"

Bernardo and Leonardo pulled Sydney up a staircase that led to the house's roof. A camera was set up on the roof, aimed toward the sky.

"Don't make too much noise," Bernardo whispered. "We are attempting to photograph God and come up with indisputable, visual proof that He truly exists."

"That's right, that's right," Leonardo added in a hush, tugging Sydney back down the stairs. "Seeing is believing. If people take our vaccine, see our shovel, and examine our photographs of God, they will have no choice but to believe. They will have full-color, living proof of God's existence.

"Right now, most people have to rely on faith to prove that He exists. But after our great scientific discoveries, they will no longer need faith—except for our artificial faith, of course. They will—"

Sydney could take it no longer. He let loose with a "hold it one second" that immediately silenced the machine-gun-mouths of Bernardo and Leonardo.

"Do you really believe that?" Sydney said. "Do you really think that 'seeing is believing'? Don't you realize that God wants us to go beyond mere sight?"

"But—"

Bernardo opened his mouth to object, but Sydney continued. "Haven't you ever stopped to wonder why God hasn't chosen to appear visually to each and every person? Don't you realize that God wants us to believe in Him as a response to His love and His Word—not simply because we can see Him with our eyes! God prefers that we exercise our faith rather than just exercise our optic nerves. There's more to life than what we can see!"

There was silence in the laboratory. Leonardo and Bernardo stood in shock, their mouths hanging open. Finally, after some uneasy seconds passed, Leonardo straightened himself up, collected his wits, and said contemptuously, "So what makes *you* the big authority on seeing and believing?"

"I'm blind," Sydney said. He turned around and groped his way toward the door.

18

EARTH'S CRAMMED WITH HEAVEN, AND EVERY COMMON BUSH AFIRE WITH GOD. AND ONLY HE WHO SEES TAKES OFF HIS SHOES, THE REST SIT ROUND AND PLUCK BLACKBERRIES.

(Elizabeth Barrett Browning)

It's amazing. People get so wrapped up looking for God's return that they fail to see His presence all around them. Not only that, but when they look for His return, they treat Him like an astronomical body as predictable as Halley's comet. For instance . . .

Jotham Cleft, a part-time prophet for the Church of Perpetual Paranoia, maintains that this time he is "very, very sure" he knows when the world is going to end and God is going to return. He tells me that a few days ago he spotted a huge "THE END" in the sky, followed by "Written and directed by God" and a long list of credits.

According to Cleft, the end of the world will occur when the planets position themselves in a straight line and several of them yell "Down in front!" Then, when the earth refuses to budge, Jupiter will explode and engulf the earth in poisonous gases and extra-hot taco sauce. The entire earth will be devoured, except for the crust.

Such predictions are not new. Many ancient forecasters treated the Messiah's first coming like a predictable bit of weather—a cold front, for example.

These forecasters forgot that "seeing God" involves so much more.

DO NOT DISTURB

About two thousand years ago, there lived a forecaster who did not like to be disturbed on a certain night of the week—the night he prepared his prophecy forecast.

On this particular night, we find him rushing and shuffling through stacks of paper and occasionally glancing at the sky for special signs. Next to him was something that looked like a weather map; he called it his "prophecy map."

"Let's see," he muttered to himself. "From my research, I'd say there is only a 15 percent chance of the Messiah arriving this week. Also, it looks as if the earth will be partly clouded with signs and wonders through tomorrow, diminishing by evening."

Suddenly, the forecaster clicked his fingers, as if an idea had just occurred to him, and he flipped through his copy of the Scriptures. .

"Just as I thought!" he declared. "Micah 5:2 says that Bethlehem will be the Messiah's birthplace. And since there are not many babies being born in Bethlehem this week, I better lower my prediction to only a 10 percent chance of seeing the Messiah."

With frantically fast fingers, he jotted some notes on a scroll and then hurried to the window for another glance at the sky. That's when there came a knock on the door.

The forecaster tried to ignore it.

There it was again. Another knock.

But the forecaster simply ignored it again.

Finally, the door squeaked open, and the forecaster's wife poked in her head. "Someone here to see you, Dear. I think it's urgent."

Do Not Disturb

The forecaster exploded. "Wife, you know better than to interrupt me when I'm getting my prophecy forecast together. I'm due to give my forecast any moment now, and I'm busy, busy, busy. Tell the person to come back some other month."

After the wife timidly backed off, the forecaster slammed the door behind her and threw himself back into his work.

Yes sir, it was prophecy time, so the forecaster wheeled his prophecy map outside onto the balcony, and he gazed at the crowd that had gathered below.

"This week, there is only a 10 percent chance of the Messiah arriving, but there will be scattered signs and wonders through tomorrow," he announced to his audience. "The prophet Isaiah says that the Messiah will be a descendant of David and that He will open the eyes of the blind, but I don't expect anyone like that to come into the world this week."

The people below appeared disappointed, but they decided to stick around for the rest of the forecast anyway.

"I also project a 30 percent chance of plagues, with lightly scattered temptations by tomorrow afternoon," the forecaster said, jabbing a pointer at his map. "Many blessings will shower down on us by tomorrow evening, but the showers will taper off toward morning. And . . ."

Just then, he was distracted by the sound of a whispered "Pssst!" It was coming from the door leading onto the balcony. Embarrassed, the forecaster told his audience "Excuse me" and went to investigate.

It was his wife again.

"Dear, you must come quick! It's an emergency! These people downstairs are—"

"If you don't stop interrupting my work, I am going to get very, very angry," the forecaster hissed, like a person who was counting to ten under his breath.

"But, Dear—"

The forecaster's wife stopped mid-sentence. She could tell by the glare in her husband's eyes that there was no convincing him. So she left, not knowing what to do, while her husband went back to his work.

* * *

It was now morning, and the forecaster was shoveling down his breakfast, looking through scrolls, and thinking about his next prophecy report. He had a busy, busy day ahead.

"I'm sorry I interrupted you last night," said his wife. "It's just that—"

"If you're sorry, then why are you interrupting me *now*?" griped the forecaster, without even looking up from the scroll he was reading. "I'm a very busy man, running this hotel and providing prophecy forecasts every week, so please leave me in peace for one morning. I've got to be alert for the Messiah, and I don't have time for this idle chatter."

"Okay, okay. I'm sorry, Dear. But aren't you even curious what that emergency was all about last night?"

"All right already," the forecaster surrendered in frustration. "If it'll make you happy, tell me what happened last night."

"A man and his pregnant wife were looking for a place to stay, and we didn't have any rooms available. But don't worry. I was able to give them a place in our stable."

"Good," grunted the forecaster, as he returned to his morning scroll.

He was a busy, busy man . . . too busy to see what the shepherds had seen.

PART SEVEN

Blessed are the peacemakers, for they will be called sons of God.

19 IN THE SPHERE OF FORGIVENESS, TOO MANY HATCHETS ARE BURIED ALIVE.

(Lem Hubbard, *Chicago Tribune*)

Like everyone else, I'm looking forward to a future of peace when the lion and the lamb will lie down together. But from all indications, that day has not arrived. In fact, a recent experiment indicated that the lion and lamb are not even capable of sharing an apartment.

"I should have known that living with a predator wouldn't work," a lamb recently told me—a lamb that made the mistake of marrying a lion because she was infatuated with his hairy chest.

According to the lamb, they are totally incompatible. She rolls up the toothpaste from the bottom while her lion spouse insists on tearing it wide open in the middle. But even more exasperating is that the lion clogs the shower drain with hair every morning, and he leaves his kills lying all around the apartment.

Evidently, the lamb has had a particularly terrible time sleeping because her husband's bedtime prayer has her terrified. The lion's routine prayer is, "Now I lay me down with sheep, I pray the Lord her soul to keep; if she is eaten before she wakes . . ."

Yes, we have a way to go before we can live at peace, for even in the church we do battle with one another. Observe . . .

I Never Promised You a Hot Tub

THE VALENTINE'S DAY MASSACRE

The gang and I were worried. Big Al Bofforanti sent one of his thugs over with a message that he wanted to meet us at Rosie's Cafe on Valentine's Day. Big Al said he had some big news.

But I thought it was a trap. Ya see, ever since Big Al and his boys split off from our church and started their own church, we've had all sorts of run-ins.

Just for starters, they kidnapped our overhead projector and said that if we didn't pay a ransom, they'd wear out its bulb or trade it in for a home computer that performed all the functions of your basic Q-tip.

Believe me, we were worried.

We decided to retaliate, though, by having one of our guys (Scratchy-Voice Moran) dress up as one of their choir members and sing off-tune during their annual Christmas pageant.

This gang warfare can sometimes get pretty low and vicious.

I suppose you're wondering how the split between my gang and Big Al's gang started. Well, I'll tell ya. Me and the boys were having a Bible study, when suddenly Big Al pointed to 2 Corinthians 6:14 ("Do not be yoked together with unbelievers") and said it means you can't be a Christian if you eat hard-boiled eggs with unbelievers.

As you might have guessed, I got hot under the collar, stepped up to Big Al, and said, "You gotta be a complete dummy to believe that 'Be not yoked with unbelievers' means you can't eat hard-boiled eggs with non-Christians. That's ridiculous.

Everyone knows that the verse means you can't eat *scrambled* eggs with unbelievers."

The whole room got real quiet-like, and Big Al just sat there cracking his knuckles and looking kinda mean. Then he said, "Ya wanna step in back and make something of it?"

So I said, "Sure," and we both grabbed our Bible dictionaries and stepped out in the alley. Right off, Big Al said that he looked up the original Greek word for *yoked* and it definitely refers to hard-boiled eggs.

But I said, "If you studied your biblical history properly, you woulda known that most early Christians only scrambled their eggs, though one sect was known to specialize in Denver omelets."

I couldn't believe that Big Al was so ignorant. So I said, "You ain't no Christian, Big Al. Leave our church."

Then Big Al said, "I'll gladly leave your church, 'cause I don't believe that *you're* a true Christian."

Well . . . ever since we broke into two gangs, I have been in for a lot of shocks. I soon found out that Big Al believes that people with bad eyesight have to install stained-glass lenses in wire-rimmed glasses, or they can't be true Christians.

Have you ever heard anything so silly? Everyone knows you can't be a Christian unless you buy stained-glass *contact lenses* on sale from the Sears Optical Service, and only if you clean them using either the right sleeve of your sweater or the very middle of a freshly washed handkerchief that has your initials on the bottom left-hand corner.

During the next few months, violence intensified. One of my brothers was eating scrambled eggs at a sidewalk cafe when a black sedan suddenly screeched to the curb. Six members of Big Al's gang rushed out of the car, sprinkling pepper and Worcestershire sauce all over the place. They knew perfectly well that my brother hates pepper and Worcestershire sauce on his eggs. How much lower could they get?

Horror followed horror. Two weeks later, I learned that Big Al's gang no longer supported what I always held to be a basic

Christian belief. They no longer believed that after four months of age, all babies must be capable of ordering out for pizza.

Finally, the big day came—Valentine's Day. I got our gang together and we went down to Rosie's Cafe to find out what Big Al wanted. We weren't there more than five minutes when Big Al, Long-Neck Lonigan, Short-Nose Newton, and several other thugs came striding into the restaurant carrying violin cases and wearing pin-striped suits.

Immediately, our gang stood up and all the customers in the restaurant ran for cover.

"Hey! Don't you dare mess up my joint!" Rosie said.

"You stay out of this!" Big Al snapped.

But Rosie wouldn't take no for an answer. She slammed down her spatula and stepped between our two gangs.

"I'm ashamed of you boys!" she shouted.

I was shocked by Rosie's boldness, but Big Al just stood there with a rock-hard expression on his scarred face. Rosie continued.

"I don't know how you came up with all these so-called laws about what you gotta do to be a true Christian. Why, I heard one of you guys tell my waitress that if she didn't give him a reduced rate on our liver-flavored waffles, God not only wouldn't love her, but he wouldn't even leave her a 15 percent tip!"

I wanted to put an end to Rosie's brashness, but Big Al held up a hand and said, "Let the little lady finish."

"God wants us to obey Him," Rosie said, "but when we stumble, He isn't waiting to clobber us! You guys seem to think that God is a big godfather gangster in the sky ready to put us in concrete shoes if we make the slightest mistake. Well, that's not true."

With these words, she gave us a long stare—kind of like the look my old Sunday school teacher used to give me whenever I messed up. Then Rosie asked if she could take our orders.

Suddenly Big Al reached for his violin case, and I ducked 'cause I thought he was going for a weapon. But instead he said,

"Ya know, I've been thinking about things lately. And Rosie's right. I say we stop the warfare."

Then, to my utter surprise, Big Al pulled a box of candy from his violin case and said, "Happy Valentine's Day, Mugsy."

Smiling, I took the candy and ordered hard-boiled eggs for everyone. The treat was on me.

20 ALL MEN DESIRE PEACE, BUT FEW DESIRE THINGS THAT MAKE FOR PEACE.

(Thomas a Kempis)

Utopias. Since the beginning of time, men and women have dreamed of creating the perfect country. The perfect city. The perfect commune.

There is only one problem. Utopians put their ultimate faith in humanity. In fact, they have so much faith in humanity, they don't even bother checking to make sure they have the right number of white pieces and coleslaw orders when leaving Kentucky Fried Chicken.

But every Utopian believer eventually discovers that humans cannot reach perfection, because every Utopia eventually fails.

For example, the Soviet Union was built on the Utopian notion that people will someday learn to live in communistic harmony. But as the Soviet Union tries to force people into its idea of perfection, it spawns intolerance and oppression.

Don't get me wrong. I'm all in favor of aiming for perfection. But when we *expect* perfection, when we forget we live in a fallen world, we can get ourselves into trouble. When we expect perfection, we get angry at the slightest imperfections. It is hard to be at peace in marriage when we expect perfection from our spouses. And it is hard to keep the peace in church when congregations expect a stained-glass Utopia.

Let me submit Exhibit A as evidence: A meal with Clifton Melbourne.

WAITER, THERE'S A FLY IN MY CHURCH

"May I take your order?" the waiter asked, leaning over the table like a tall, thin, elm tree bending in the wind.

"Uh . . . yes, I think I *am* ready to order," said Clifton Melbourne, scanning the menu one last time. "I'd like your church of the day."

Muttering "uh-huh," the waiter scribbled into his note pad. "And how would you like your church?"

"Medium rare, please."

"All righty." (Scribble, scribble, scribble.)

After an exchange of courtesies, the waiter vanished into the kitchen, and Clifton began sampling offerings at the Sunday school salad bar. He tried a small part of an Ephesians study, and he heaped on a generous portion of a class entitled, "A Biblical Study of Waterskiing."

All was going well, almost too well, when it happened. The waiter returned with the main-course church, and Clifton took a taste.

"I can't accept this church!" he exploded. "It's lukewarm and the sermons are so bland that I'd have to drink a gallon of coffee to keep from falling asleep. Don't you have a church that has a little more get up and go—a little more spark?"

"You mean you want your church well-done?" asked the waiter, trying to contain his irritation.

"Yes, that's it. Well-done."

"As you wish, sir."

About fifteen minutes later, the waiter arrived with the next church—a dish that was steaming and bubbling and boiling over. "Now *that's* what I call a church!" Clifton exclaimed.

However, his optimism did not last long. It took only one minute for Clifton to transform back into an angry customer.

"I asked for a well-done church, not an *overdone* church," he said. "I like churches that are on fire, but this is going too far. This church is so spicy and wild that even the dinner rolls are rolling in the aisles!"

Angrily snapping open the menu and scouring its pages once more, Clifton decided that what he really wanted was a cozy, comfortable church. Nothing so exotic.

"Very well, sir."

Fifteen minutes passed before the waiter returned. And was Clifton satisfied this time? Not on your life.

"This church may be cozy, but it's much too small. I want my money's worth. What are you trying to do? Rip me off?"

Obediently, the waiter took away the tiny, cozy congregation and returned with a large church—a family-sized serving. It was a huge concoction, spilling over the edges of the plate.

"How do you expect me to handle such a large church?" Clifton gasped. "I could get lost in a church that big. Look! I just dropped my silverware and it vanished into the huge church. No sir, this congregation is too sprawling and impersonal. Besides, the services are too long. I couldn't handle it all in one sitting."

"You could try taking part of the sermon home with you in a doggy bag."

"No thanks. Hey, do you got a church that is really 'with it'? You know, a real trendy church."

In a matter of minutes, the waiter was back with a serving of church a la mode, but Clifton found this modern congregation too fluffy and flaky. "It's also so shallow that there's nothing to sop up with my bread."

The next church was a nondenominational dish, Ecumenical Goulash, but Clifton's assessment was "too untraditional." He wanted a church that had a long history, a church that had been simmering for centuries.

That's why the waiter brought out a more traditional church; but after a few tastes, Clifton declared that it was too rigid and stale. So the waiter tried another mainline course, but this one was too fattening and too rich.

"Actually, I'd really like to sink my teeth into some intellectual debates. Do you have a church with brains? That's what I'd like!"

No, it wasn't. When the waiter returned with an intellectual church, Clifton said it tasted more like spaghetti and meatheads.

On and on it went. Clifton called the next church too phony, for it had too many artificial members. But the "all-natural" church wasn't what he wanted either. "I'm allergic to all-natural churches," he pointed out. "When I attend one of those, I break out in a rash of impatience and disagreements."

Finally, after the next offering was labeled "too syrupy sweet," the waiter brought out the final church on the menu and slammed it on the table. Then he looked at Clifton with a glare that was hot enough to roast a ham faster than any microwave.

"Excuse me, Sir, but I can't keep quiet any longer," the waiter said through gritted teeth. "I wonder whether *anything* is going to satisfy you. You fail to recognize a simple, basic lesson taught to us by Christ—people are imperfect. And since the church is made up of people, it too is imperfect."

"Oh, I agree," Clifton said. "All of the churches that you've shown me have problems you wouldn't believe. They are as imperfect as—"

"What I'm trying to say is that if churches are imperfect, why do you demand *perfection*? Why? Tell me why?"

The waiter paused, hoping for a sensible answer, but Clifton's mind was elsewhere. He was busily examining the latest church that had been brought out.

"You know, this church is much too divisive," he said. "It's broken up into all sorts of tiny chunks, and if I tried mixing them up, they'd probably start fighting and give me indigestion. I really wish people would just learn to control their bickering. Gripe, gripe, gripe."

Exasperated, the waiter said nothing but simply turned and marched away.

"Oh, how rude," Clifton said as he headed for the exit without leaving a tip. "I must say that I'm terribly disappointed in this establishment. The waiter was unfriendly, the service was slow, the lighting was much too dark, the chairs were a little hard, the silverware was spotted, the tablecloths were . . ."

Blah, blah, blah.

21 A "BIT OF LOVE" IS THE ONLY BIT THAT WILL BRIDLE THE TONGUE. (Fred Beck)

Winston Churchill was not only well-known for leading Britain through World War II. He was also well-known for his ability to mobilize an army of words in verbal battles. Case in point:

Lady Astor: Winston, if you were my husband, I should flavor your coffee with poison.

Churchill: Madam, if I were your husband, I should drink it.

In the war of words, insults such as these are the verbal equivalent of conventional weapons—weapons wielded by opponents who look each other in the eye. Gossip, on the other hand, is the verbal equivalent of a terrorist's bomb.

Like the terrorist, the gossip doesn't face his victim. He skulks off in secret and plants gossip in the minds of another person—like a terrorist planting a bomb in a car. Then the gossip slips away and waits for his words to do the damage.

This isn't to say that insults are a legitimate form of verbal warfare just because they're delivered in person. They can do just as much harm. The point is that gossip can explode in a victim's face without a moment's warning, and without leaving any clue as to who the enemy is. But where there's a victim, there's usually a detective. Sherlock Holmes, perhaps?

THE CASE OF THE POISONED TONGUE

"I suppose you're wondering why I asked all of you here," said Detective Sherlock Holmes, peering at each person one by one. "Before this night ends, I will identify the murderer!"

A gasp passed from person to person, circling the room twice before Holmes got upset and told them to stop gasping.

While everyone sat at the edge of their seats, the famous detective paced the room and reviewed the three murders that had occurred.

The first victim, Dr. Phelps, was a very generous man. According to his wife, "My husband was always willing to drop his work to help a friend. Of course, that usually bothered his patients who were left on the operating table."

"Aha!" shouted Watson, Holmes's assistant. "Maybe one of the doctor's angry patients shot him!"

"Shot him?" said Holmes. "Dr. Phelps has not been shot! He has been stabbed in the back by gossip and lies."

"My goodness, you're right, Holmes!" Watson turned the victim over and saw a string of words sticking out of Dr. Phelps's back. Someone had been talking behind the doctor's back, knifing him with gossip and nasty remarks. The words had pierced his heart.

"As it says in the Good Book," Holmes noted, " 'With the tongue we praise our Lord and Father, and with it we curse men.' Yes, the tongue can be used in wonderful ways; but it also can cut like a knife."

Only days after the doctor was back-stabbed, co-workers found the second victim—Mrs. Gregory, the historian. According to the autopsy report, she had been poisoned by a four-letter word, which doctors found lodged in her throat. Police reports revealed that Mrs. Gregory had quarreled with somebody on the morning of her death.

"As the Good Book says," recited Holmes, " 'No man can tame the tongue. It is a restless evil, full of deadly poison.' "

The third victim, a Spanish immigrant, might have been murdered by the "Unwelcome Wagon"—an unfriendly counterpart to the "Welcome Wagon."

The Unwelcome Wagon holds notorious housewarming parties for new immigrants. Unfortunately, this ruthless organization's idea of a housewarming is to set fire to the immigrant's house.

The Spanish immigrant in this case, however, hadn't been killed by an ordinary fire. He had been burned by the flames of racial jokes.

"As the Good Book says," Holmes recited, " 'The tongue is a fire, a world of evil among the parts of the body.' "

Once again looking at the suspects who had gathered in his office, the detective boldly stated, "I think there is a common link between all three murders!"

Another gasp passed from person to person. By this time, everybody was so far over the edge of their seats, most of them were sitting on air.

Was the murderer Mrs. White, who hated historians, made racial jokes, and was a patient of Dr. Phelps? Was it Mr. Green, who was jealous of historians, hated doctors, and served as treasurer of the local Unwelcome Wagon? Was it Colonel Mustard, who believed immigrants should be shipped home, thought historians were stupid, and told more lies than truth? Or was it . . . ?

Sherlock Holmes had a plan. He had asked Watson to leave the room unnoticed and to turn off the lights at midnight. Holmes was sure that in the darkness the true murderer would try to escape. When the lights came back on, they would know who did it.

Holmes was at his eloquent best. When the lights went

off, the room filled with the sound of banging doors, scuffling feet, shouting voices, and people bumping into each other.

When the lights came back on, the room was *empty*. Everyone had fled—even Sherlock Holmes!

Watson stumbled back into the room, confused by what had happened. "Where in the world did Holmes run off to?" he muttered.

Then he saw a note posted on the mantlepiece.

> My dear Watson, you're probably wondering why everybody fled. Well, I'll tell you. In our hearts, we *all* murder people with our words. We hurt others with our lies, our fury, our profanity, our gossip, and our back-stabbing. As the Good Book says, we are *all* guilty. That is why all of us fled. But fear not. The Good Book also says we will be redeemed if we know where to flee to. So take heart!
>
> Your friend,
> Sherlock Holmes

When Watson finished reading the note, he realized that he too was guilty. He too had hurt others with his tongue.

Dropping the note, Watson picked up his cane, threw on his cape, flung open the door, and fled into the open arms of Jesus.

PART EIGHT

Blessed are those who are persecuted because of righteousness, for theirs is the kingdom of heaven.

22 CHRISTIANS AND NON-CHRISTIANS HAVE SOMETHING IN COMMON: WE'RE BOTH UPTIGHT ABOUT EVANGELISM.

(Rebecca Manley Pippert)

When it comes to evangelism, many Christians try so hard to appear *not* pushy that they almost apologize for their beliefs. In fact, I wouldn't be surprised if somebody someday suggests that the Apostle's Creed should read this way:

"I hate to force my beliefs on you, but if you don't mind, I think I believe in God the Father almighty (or at least some vague Being, depending on your viewpoint, which I'm sure is sincere), Maker of heaven and earth or evolver of heaven and earth, depending on whether you side with creationists or evolutionists, both of which have interesting points and are very sincere. . . ."

Fortunately, we haven't gone this far. But, unfortunately, many of us *have* toned down our witness because we're afraid of rejection. We're no longer afraid of being tossed to the lions, but we *are* afraid of being tossed to our society's psychological lions.

The solution is simple. We need to be ourselves and stop treating evangelism like a contest out of "Wide World of Witnessing."

What is "Wide World of Witnessing"? I'm glad you asked.

HONK IF YOU LOVE JESUS
JESUS SAVES
JESUS SAVES
HOLY BIBLE

"WIDE WORLD OF WITNESSING"

HOWARD: Welcome to "Wide World of Witnessing," the show that captures the thrill of evangelism and the agony of rebuke! This is Howard Hardsell . . .

DON: And Dandy Deacon Don . . .

HOWARD: Speaking to you from Madison Share Garden in New York where a kneeling-room-only crowd has come to witness the 1987 indoor/outdoor tract meet—an evangelism contest pitting the Concordia Concordances against the defending world champions, the Narnia Lions. Tell me, Don, with this being the season opener, how do the two teams size up?

DON: I'll tell you, Howard, the Concordances looked strong in pre-season evangelism. They've really benefited from the recent trade that brought Jeff Groffke from the Hartford Hymnals in return for two youth ministers, a future draft pick, an undisclosed amount of prayers, and six boxes of choir cleats. The Lions, on the other hand, always provide nail-tough competition. The major problem is that their star evangelist, Bill Winters, has been on the disabled list since he broke his ankle while backsliding.

HOWARD: Well . . . at least the Lions managed to negotiate a contract with their star deaconess, Martha Quest.

DON: That's true, Howard. Quest was pleased with her whopping seven-digit salary. But she would've been even more pleased if two of the digits hadn't been on the wrong side of the decimal point.

HOWARD: Okay, the game is about to begin and the excitement is really thick. Wouldn't you say it's thick, Don?

DON: Yes, Howard, really thick.

HOWARD: There's the tip-off, and the two teams have begun to evangelize! A pair of Lions—I think it's the duo of Simpson and Barnes—have approached an unsuspecting person and are doing a nice job of explaining the gospel.

DON: Yes, Howard, but, if I'm not mistaken, Simpson and Barnes are showing their usual weakness. They're laying out the importance of becoming a Christian, but they're failing to show even the slightest interest in the person they're talking to. They keep addressing him as "Occupant."

HOWARD: I think you're right, Don. The person is clearly offended by Simpson and Barnes's technique and probably feels like another faceless person on an evangelistic assembly line.

DON: I guess it's such offensive behavior that earned Simpson the 1986 Offensive Player of the Year award.

HOWARD: Now, the evangelism is really picking up on the field and the Narnia Lions are going for the conversion. But, what's this? I can't believe it! Strauss is offering no follow-up at all.

DON: That may be a costly error, Howard. Strauss found someone who was sincerely interested in the Lord, but all he did was stuff tracts in the fellow's pockets.

HOWARD: Hit-and-run evangelism, wouldn't you say?

DON: You got it, Howard. Strauss fumbled the opportunity to make sure the person got involved in a church where a new believer grows.

HOWARD: Meanwhile, the Concordances are dropping memory verses from the tops of buildings; Strauss is still stuffing tracts into people's pockets; Nat Perkins is leading interference while Greg Thomas plasters bumper stickers on people's foreheads, and . . . yes, it looks like there's a flag on the play!

DON: Howard, I think the Lions' Wally Eckstrom has been called for illegal use of Christian jargon.

HOWARD: I bet you're right, Don. Eckstrom is known for using so much Christian terminology that most non-Christians don't know what he's talking about unless they have a translator handy.

DON: Well, I certainly called that one right. It appears that Eckstrom went up to a non-Christian and said, "I bet you'd like to be washed in the blood of the Lamb because when you get into the Word you can see that it overflows with grace. And if you'd let Jesus into your heart, you could be sanctified, redeemed, justified, and you would really bless me because I'm responding to the 'feed-My-sheep' exhortation and I really think you'd be blessed by daily quiet times."

The medics are tending to the non-Christian who is down on the field. Most likely, he sprained his brain trying to figure out what all of those terms meant.

HOWARD: Well, Don, I guess it's another poor start for Eckstrom because he's just been benched for the rest of the game. Eckstrom hasn't had a decent season since 1981, when he led the league in souls-batted-in.

But back to the action. The Narnia Lions have jumped to a four–two lead in converts, and I think the Concordances' problem is that they seem a little fearful of talking about the Lord.

DON: Yes, the Concordances had the same problem last year. They seem afraid to express their Christian beliefs because they don't want to offend anyone. The Lions, on the other hand, have the opposite problem. They not only fail to show sensitivity to non-Christians, but they give the impression that Christianity chiefly consists of a series of "don'ts." Don't dance, don't drink, don't smoke.

HOWARD: Good observation, Dandy. If I'm not mistaken, the Lions' assistant manager is the one who coached the "smoking topic" to the number one position in both the U.P.I. and A.P. rankings of the world's worst sins last year.

DON: That's right, Howard. Some sin analysts even believe that this year the smoking issue may become the first issue to win the grand slam. In other words, it may be named the worst sin in North America, Western Europe, Eastern Europe, and Wheaton College. It's just too bad they don't put more energy into the more devious sins, such as pride and greed.

HOWARD: Just a second, Don! The Concordances are trying to turn things around by putting in their ace relief preacher, Tod Johnson, who has been warming up in the bullpen.

Meanwhile, the Lions squad is beginning to tire, except for Harvey Tinsel. He's the former used-car salesman whose over-commercialization of the gospel might make him a top candidate for this year's Offensive Player of the Year.

DON: That's right, Howard.

HOWARD: Thanks, Don.

DON: Don't mention it, Howard.

HOWARD: I already *did* mention it, Don.

DON: Why do we keep repeating each other's names, Howard?

HOWARD: Good question, Don. Okay, we're into the final minute, the Concordances have evened the score, and the crowd is on its feet! Streckman hands off some tracts to Tinberg, who cuts across the field, while the Lions intercept a few men on bicycles.

Simpson and Barnes still haven't asked anyone's name, Groffke is handing out handkerchiefs and telling people to "honk if you love Jesus," and Strauss has just set a new world's record by stuffing 1,420 tracts into one person's shirt pocket! And . . . yes . . . I do believe . . . yes, there's the final buzzer and the Concordances have themselves a come-from-behind, upset victory over the Lions, six to five! A real season-opening thriller. Wouldn't you say this was a thriller, Don?

DON: Yes, Howard, a real thriller.

HOWARD: Now, stay tuned for the post-game show when our roving reporter talks to the coaches and the players. And don't forget to tune in next week when "Wide World of Witnessing" takes you on an exciting deep-sea fisher-of-men expedition off the coast of Trinity Seminary. Until then, this is Howard Hardsell . . .

DON: And Dandy Deacon Don . . .

HOWARD: Saying good night.

23 EVERYONE SEEMS TO CRAVE THE ANESTHETIZING SECURITY OF BEING IDENTIFIED WITH THE MAJORITY.

(Martin Luther King, Jr.)

In his book *The Gulag Archipelago,* Alexander Solzhenitsyn tells about a communist conference in the 1920s where someone suggested an ovation for Soviet leader Joseph Stalin. Immediately, everybody was up to his feet, applauding wildly.

There was only one problem. Who would have the nerve to be the first one to *stop* applauding? After all, if you stopped applauding first, wouldn't that mean you were not loyal to Comrade Stalin? Wouldn't that mean you had a mind of your own?

The applause went on. As Solzhenitsyn put it, "With make-believe enthusiasm on their faces, looking at each other with faint hope, the district leaders were just going to go on and on applauding till they fell where they stood, till they were carried out of the hall on stretchers!"

Finally, after eleven minutes of solid applause, the director of a local paper factory decided that enough was enough. He stopped clapping and sat down.

That night, the factory owner was arrested.

Today, we don't face the type of persecution that a nonconformist in Soviet society faced then or faces now. But we still encounter subtle forms of pressure—pressures that try to mold us into society's preselected shapes.

And speaking of pressures, it's time to tune in to the latest pressure-packed episode of everyone's favorite television series—"Church Trek."

CHURCH TREK

Church. The final frontier. These are the voyages of the Church Bus Enterprise. Its five-year mission: To explore strange, new denominations; to seek out new Sunday school materials; to boldly go where no Bible study has gone before!

Star date 4046.2. It was an ordinary day on the Church Bus Enterprise with the crew relaxing and playing horseshoes. The only thing out of the ordinary was that Dr. McCoy forgot to take the shoes off the horse before we started the game.

Suddenly, an overly loud soundtrack began playing dramatic music and we received a distress signal from a nearby planet. Putting the ship in Scotty's command, Mr. Spock and I decided to beam down to the planet to investigate.

But it was a bad choice. When we beamed down, we found ourselves in a prison cell, standing next to a two-headed creature.

"Quick Scotty!" I shouted into my communication device. "Beam us back up!"

"No! Wait!" shouted one of the creature's two heads—a head we later found out was named Jack. "I'm the one who sent the distress signal, and you've got to help me!"

According to the creature, he was being imprisoned for breaking the planet's Law of Conformity—a law that says you must go along with the wishes of the planet's rulers or you will be executed.

"Don't listen to this wimp," said the creature's second head—named Clifton. "Thanks to Jack, I'm about to be executed for something I didn't do. I didn't break our planet's Law of

Conformity. But just because my head is connected to the same body as his, I'm going to be executed, too."

When I asked if there was hope for escape, Jack said they had already tried it. Just yesterday they slipped over the wall and tried to escape on a bicycle, but they didn't get very far.

"Maybe it was because we were trying to escape on an exercycle," Jack said.

Suddenly, dramatic music tipped me off that something bad was about to happen. But before I was able to react, somebody hit me on the back of the head and my mind went blank (or at least blanker than it usually is).

Star date 4046.3. When I came to, Mr. Spock and I were tied to chairs while a four-headed creature interrogated our new friend, the two-headed creature.

"We have ways of making you *stop* talking," snarled the four-headed beast, pointing a hot lamp in Jack's face.

Slowly, I learned what was going on. The rulers of this planet did not think people should talk about God in public. They thought God was a private matter. God's place was in the home, not in the workplace. Not in the schools. Not in the offices.

In fact, the only time you were allowed to pray in public on this planet was when you did it in Morse code by clacking your teeth together. But Jack did not abide by this restriction. He openly spoke about God.

The rulers of this planet also believed that the more modern an idea was, the better it was. If an idea was five minutes old, they thought it was better than an idea that was ten minutes old. Therefore, because the existence of God was an old, old belief, they discarded it like a disposable towel.

Even the original theory of evolution was now considered out-of-date. People here believed in a *new* theory of evolution in which Stone Age apes sat around waiting for each other to evolve—a practice that soon inspired the saying, "A watched ape never evolves."

An even more recent theory, formulated about five seconds ago, suggested that teenaged apes used to come home and announce, "I'm evolving," to which the father would bellow, "Not in my house you're not!"

But I'm getting off the subject. The point is that Jack was considered out-of-date. So the rulers decided to execute both him—and us. (Dramatic music.)

Star date 4046.4. Before we were to be executed, the rulers wanted to try one other strategy to get Jack to conform. They took Mr. Spock, myself, and the two-headed creature to a hospital.

"What's happening now?" I whispered to Jack.

"I don't think you want to know," said Jack's other head, Clifton. But when I insisted, Clifton told me they were taking us to the hospital's most feared unit.

"You've heard of intensive care units, haven't you?" Clifton said. "Well, this is an intensive *careless* unit—where nurses accidentally drop you off of exam tables and mistakenly plug you into the wrong monitors."

The room they placed us in was occupied by at least fourteen other creatures. And the creature in the bed next to me was screaming in pain.

I leaned over to Jack. "What's wrong with that guy?"

"The nurses are forcing him to wear a Walkman headphone all day and listen to Top 40 music."

Sure enough, the nurses were surgically attaching a pair of Walkman headphones to the poor guy's head. This was all part of the plot.

"We're told that God should remain a very private affair, only to be thought about during our quiet moments with ourselves," Jack whispered to me. "But the catch is, they never allow us to have private moments alone. They're always filling our ears with noise, so people never have a chance to think about God."

That was true, I observed. On this planet, if you weren't listening to Walkman radios, you probably were rooted in front of a VCR or playing video games.

For a small fee, you could even hook your brain into cable TV so television shows could be broadcast directly into your thoughts. Then, if you wanted to change the channel, you simply tugged on your earlobe.

Star date 4046.5. It was execution day. Mr. Spock, myself, and our two-headed friend were lined up against a wall, waiting to be shot by a laser-equipped firing squad.

"For my sake, please give in to the Law of Conformity!" Clifton shouted at his other head, Jack.

"No," Jack responded, "I'm more than willing to die as a martyr."

"But what about me? I don't want to be a martyr. Do you have a black belt in stupidity or what? This is our last chance. Conform to the rulers' wishes and let us live!"

Jack still would not alter his convictions. The rulers of this planet had tried to convince him that right and wrong were values that changed according to the time of day. They had tried to convince him that God was more like a Nerf ball than a solid rock.

But Jack couldn't swallow their arguments, even if he had an ocean to wash them down with.

"Do you have any last requests?" said our executioner. "Would you like a blindfold?"

"No, I would not like a blindfold," Jack said firmly, while Clifton began to whimper.

That's when Mr. Spock had an idea, a brilliant idea. "Yes, I *would* like a blindfold!" he announced. "But I would like the blindfolds to be placed over the eyes of the firing squad."

"Huh?"

"You wouldn't deny the request of a man about to be executed, would you?"

Unsure about proper firing squad etiquette, the captain of the guard reluctantly agreed to blindfold both himself and the firing squad. Consequently, when he shouted, "Fire!" the squad didn't know in which direction to shoot.

While they stumbled over each other, I snatched my communication device from the captain of the guard's back pocket and we hurdled the brick wall. Then we slipped into an enemy storage room and I signaled the Church Bus Enterprise.

"Beam us up, Scotty!"

Star date 4046.9. Mr. Spock and I were sitting in the back of the church bus. I was in a philosophical mood while Mr. Spock was in the mood to scrape twenty-year-old gum wads from the bottoms of the bus chairs.

It had now been four days since we had made our escape. But I was still amazed to think about what had happened when we beamed back to the Church Bus Enterprise—Jack's two-headed body had divided into two *separate* bodies. Finally, he was freed from Clifton.

"Talk about using peer pressure," I said to Mr. Spock. "When you have to share the same body with another head, there can be intense pressure to conform. But now that Jack is his own person, he has no need to conform."

"Correction, Captain Kirk," said Mr. Spock as he used his laser to dissolve wads of gum under the seats. "Jack knows there is no such thing as a nonconformist. We *all* conform to something. Jack simply chooses to conform to God's wishes, rather than the wishes of his planet's rulers."

"Okay, you got a point there. But at least it is safe to say that Jack was freed from having to share a body with another head. He's his own person. He's independent, a lone ranger, a—"

"Correction," Mr. Spock said as he taped a stick of dynamite to the bottom of a chair. (Sometimes you have to use drastic measures to remove solidified gum.) "Jack knows that we are all connected to the same body. We're connected to a spiritual body. A body of believers. There's no such thing as a lone ranger."

I paused and sighed. "Okay, you got a point there," I said. "But at least it's safe to say that I have two feet."

"You won't be able to say that for long if you don't stop poking at my stick of dynamite with your toes."

I glanced down at the dynamite and gasped. Then, with

dramatic music flooding my ears, I dove for cover and the dynamite detonated with a tearing roar.

When the smoke cleared, Mr. Spock and I saw that the dynamite had done its job. It had torn a thick wad of gum from the bottom of the seat and hurtled it into space.

The gum eventually developed its own orbit around the sun and later became known as Halley's comet. But that's another story.

24

THE MIND IS ITS OWN PLACE, AND IN ITSELF CAN MAKE A HEAVEN OF HELL, A HELL OF HEAVEN. (John Milton)

To treat severe cases of epilepsy, doctors sometimes separate the left half of the brain from the right half, producing what is called a "split brain." Many split-brain patients suffer only subtle side-effects, but that is not always the case. One patient, for example, says that after she is fully dressed her left hand may reach into the closet, grab a pair of shorts she does not want to wear, and put them on over her other pair.

This type of split brain is an unfortunate reality for some, but there is another type of split brain that we should not tolerate. It occurs when we live one way in one environment and another way in another environment. In *The Gravedigger File,* Os Guinness notes that in our fragmented, modular society, a person may have a *multiply* fragmented mind. We may have "one mind for church, another for the classroom, one for reading the Bible, another for reading the newspaper, one for the world of the family, another for the world of business."

What does all of this have to do with persecution? you ask. Let me tell you. Imitating Jesus in *all* spheres of our experience can result in some unpleasant confrontations and uncomfortable predicaments. It is safer and easier to leave God boxed-in at home when we venture into the world.

But although leaving God at home may eliminate confrontations, it can also lead to a pretty dull existence. Besides, it makes about as much sense as having a left hand that is at odds with the rest of the body.

THERE'S A LION IN MY MIND

The guide gathered his group of tourists together and pointed to a narrow crack that ran down the middle of a gray landscape. "That, folks, is what separates the left brain from the right brain."

Mr. Updike, one of the tourists, was thrilled. It wasn't every day that he toured an actual brain. He asked his wife and kids to pose by the narrow gorge; and after twenty minutes of focusing, he clicked a dozen photographs and ran off a roll of movie film.

As the group marched through the inner rooms of the brain, the guide explained that the right brain is the center of creativity. It is the realm of music, art, imagination, and insight.

"The left brain," he added, "is the more analytical portion of the brain—the center for science, numbers, reasoning, and language. Next, moving along to our left, you will see—"

"Just one minute," said Mrs. Abington, a tourist who was poring over a map of the brain. "What about religion? Where is the center of a person's spiritual nature?"

The guide shot the question down with a scowl. "You're *not* allowed to ask questions until I give permission. Understand?"

Mrs. Abington nodded, and the guide's frown snapped back into a fixed smile. "Okay, folks, let's proceed," he said.

The group moved into the complicated inner hub of the brain where thoughts came in from every part of the mind. It was like Grand Central Station and O'Hare Airport all wrapped in one, with busy brain cells sifting through the frenzy of information.

The guide patiently waited for Mr. Updike to click off fourteen photographs of his family standing next to a stray thought and ten photographs of little Timmy pointing at a daydream. Then they filed from the brain's main terminal and into a narrow hallway.

"Now follow me," the guide said. But when he turned a corner, he stopped in his tracks. "Oops. Wrong hall."

Along this narrow passageway, hundreds of men in white uniforms were scrubbing the walls of the brain. Mrs. Abington marched up to one of the workers and asked what he was doing.

"You can't talk to the workers!" shouted the guide, tugging at Mrs. Abington's arm. "This hallway is off-limits to tourists. I think that—"

Mrs. Abington yanked loose from the guide and stormed back up to one of the workers. "You're a brainwasher, aren't you?"

"Yes, Ma'am," said the worker, tipping his hat. "My boss says I should scrub away all the religion I can find. He says that—"

"Now see here," interrupted the guide, but the worker continued anyway.

"My boss said that if he finds one smudge of spirituality in this part of the brain, he'll dock us a week's pay. Yes, Ma'am, I wash brains all right, but I don't do windows. Here's my card."

Before Mrs. Abington could take his card, the tour guide pulled her down the hall and into another region of the brain. The rest of the tour group followed close behind.

When they finally came to rest in the medulla oblongata, Mrs. Abington caught her breath and said, "You're trying to rid the brain of religion, aren't you?"

"Not true," snapped the guide. "We have no intention of eliminating religion, and I have proof."

Hiking through a tangle of nerve cells and following a path to the lower reaches of the cerebellum, the guide brought his group before a small door.

"Behind this door," he said, "you'll find faith in God. You'll find proof that we *didn't* try to destroy religion."

"Okay, so maybe you didn't destroy religion," Mrs. Abington grumbled. "But you've imprisoned it in a forgotten basement of the brain, and that's not much better!"

"That's a lie."

"It is not. You've locked up faith like a caged lion in a zoo. I bet that the only time you pay attention to your faith is when you visit it once a week on Sundays . . . when you take a Sunday stroll through your brain's zoo and gawk at your caged lion."

"Lies!"

"God doesn't want us to bury our faith in the bottom of our minds. He wants our faith to run free."

"This is great!" shouted Mr. Updike, who was happily snapping photograph after photograph of the hostile debate.

"Okay, okay, you're right!" the tour guide angrily conceded. "I admit that I *do* believe in the separation of church and state of mind. But I have a good reason. I think religion serves no function in today's world. It's better kept in a basement."

"That's the stupidest thing I've heard yet," countered Mrs. Abington. "First our modern world paved over God's creation and drove many of His animals into extinction. And now it's trying to pave over man's spiritual nature and drive faith into extinction."

"Hold that pose!" Mr. Updike shouted, after he reloaded his camera. "Yell 'cheese.' "

"Listen, Lady," the tour guide said, "if we let faith out of its cage, we'd have nothing but trouble."

"Oh, I get it. You're afraid that if you let your faith affect the entire brain, you'll have to make changes. You won't be able to justify cheating, gossiping, lusting—"

"That's right, Lady! I want my brain to be free to do what it chooses. There's nothing wrong with that!"

"Well, I'm not going to let you keep faith in a cage any longer." Mrs. Abington rushed for the basement door and tried to open it. But the guide sprang for a lever on the wall, setting off a siren that brought armed guards from all sides.

Kicking and screaming, Mrs. Abington was dragged away.

When the dust cleared, the tour guide smoothed out his uniform and put on a big smile. "Let's see, folks, where was I? Oh, yes. As I was saying, the left brain and the right brain . . ."

When the guide and his little collection of tourists had shuffled off, Mr. Updike and his family popped out from their hiding place behind some neurons. Mr. Updike looked to the left. He looked to the right. Then slowly, carefully, he eased open the door leading to the basement where faith was hidden.

For the first two seconds, he was greeted by silence. Then a rumble echoed up from the dungeon floor, followed by a few piercing points of light. A great fire of light exploded in front of Mr. Updike's eyes, and a huge lion leaped from the glow, with sparks showering from its mane like a miniature meteor storm.

"This is fantastic!" gasped Mr. Updike, as he fell to the floor and filmed the entire scene. "This will be my greatest home movie ever." (It would have been even greater had Mr. Updike remembered to remove the lens cap from his camera.)

The lion jumped over Mr. Updike's head and bounded down the corridors, shedding its glow into every cell, into every living particle of the brain.

The Lion of Judah was on the loose.